Ignited to Serve

A Collaboration Presented by:
Apostle Deborah Allen and Dr. Pamela Henkel

© 2022 Apostle Deborah Allen | Dr. Pamela Henkel

Book Cover Design: Dr. Shadaria Allison | Nichol LeAnn Perricci

Interior Book Design & Formatting: TamikaINK.com

Editor: TamikaINK.com

ALL RIGHTS RESERVED. No part of this book may be reproduced in any written, electronic, recording, or photocopying without written permission of the publisher or author. The exception would be in the case of brief quotations embodied in critical articles or reviews and pages where permission is specifically granted by the publisher or author.

LEGAL DISCLAIMER. Although the author has made every effort to ensure that the information in this book was correct at press time, the author do not assume hereby disclaim any liability to any party for loss, damage, or disruption caused by errors or missions, whether such errors or omissions result from negligence, accident, or any other cause.

Published By: Igniting The Flame Publishing

Library of Congress Cataloging-in-Publication Data has been applied for

ISBN:

PRINTED IN THE UNITED STATES OF AMERICA

Acknowledgments

Co-Visionary Author
Apostle Deborah Allen

Tadah! Hence this anthology is a mighty testament to the global movement that has erupted in my life and the lives of countless others.

I'm grateful for all the support and love that has been so graciously shown to me throughout the years. Kudos and a special thanks to Fierce Tv (viewers) and The Fierce, Ignition & Activation Show/Podcast (listeners). Please know I am forever grateful!

I serve in ministry with a mighty man of valor, Apostle Glen Allen Sr, who has embraced the fierceness in me. Lighthouse Apostolic Ministries of God Church "The House of The Prophets" a sincere thank you for always being a place of advancement, change, purpose, vision, love even dreams.

Wondrously, I have birthed six children, but I'm the mother of nine. Our children have been a blessing to my very existence. I'm so awed by my support from family, friends, and clients. All your love has been priceless. You have been the "why" inside of me!

Apostle Deborah Allen

Acknowledgments

From Co-Visionary Author
Dr. Pamela Henkel

First, I would like to thank Jesus for igniting me to serve!

Next, I would like to thank...

My wonderful husband, James. For being my constant source of joy. Our six beautiful children and our "grand" are all the apples of my eye. My mother, Constance, for always demonstrating true strength. Because of her, I have learned what it means to endure like a soldier. My earthly father and my mother in love who are cheering me on from Heaven.

Bob, my father in love who is one of my greatest teachers.

Thank you to my mentors, Les Brown, Jon Talarico, Bob Proctor, Ian Harvey, Terri Savelle Foy, and Reverend Jen Tringale. You are fixtures in my life. Thank you to my pastor, Donato Perricci, and my prayer partner Lisa Walker.

I would like to thank each Woman of Power represented in this book. Your stories have touched my heart and empowered my soul. It is an honor to be represented on the pages of this book with you! Together we will Ignite the world!

A BIG Thank You to my Visionary Partner, Apostle Deborah Allen. It has been such a joy to run alongside your vision during this anthology. I am forever grateful for this opportunity.

Thank you to the entire Anthology Team - Nichol Perricci, Dawn Lieck, Shadaria Alison, Tamika, Jaresha Moore, and Renee Huffman. Where would I be without you? Thank you for making this entire journey seamless.

My biggest takeaway from this anthology is this; when you tell God you are ready, get ready. He will make sure you have everything you need and more.

I LOVE YOU ALL

Be enthusiastic to serve the Lord, keeping your passion for Him boiling hot! Radiate with the glow of the Holy Spirit and let Him fill you with excitement as you serve Him.
Romans 12:11

To Your Greatness
BLESSINGS
Dr. Pamela Henkel

Table of Contents

FOREWORD: AN INTERVIEW BY JARESHA MOORE 1

INTRODUCTION BY APOSTLE DEBORAH ALLEN 15

INTRODUCTION BY CO-VISIONARY AUTHOR DR. PAMELA HENKEL 22

I THINK I CAN! (BUT CAN I REALLY?) BY DAWN LIECK 27

BORN TO SERVE BY DR. RENEE HUFFMAN 33

EMPOWERED TO SERVE BY JARESHA MOORE 42

EMBRACING OUR STRENGTHS BY JODIE SOLBERG 51

THE EMANCIPATION OF SHAME BY ANGELA BENNETT 62

HOPE AGAINST HOPE: GREEN LIGHT GRACE

BY SHERVONDALINE S. BREEDLOVE 73

GLOW IN THE DARK BY JASBEEN SINGH 85

I'VE GOT WHAT YOU NEED; YOU JUST DON'T KNOW IT YET.

BY APOSTLE VALERIE DAVIS 97

IT'S ALWAYS DARKEST BEFORE THE DAWN BY SUSAN HALL 105

THE POWER OF YOU! BY VALILA WILSON 111

SET ON FIRE BY LATISHA SHEARER 123

CHOOSE YOUR BEST LIFE BY CAROLYN BROOKS-COLLINS 132

LEARNING TO SERVE FROM NOTHING BY CHARISSE BURTON 142

STOP FUNCTIONING – START DANCING THROUGH YOUR LIFE AND LIVE

YOUR DREAMS! BY ELLEN WULFERT 154

WHAT LIT MY FIRE TO SERVE LIFE'S NOW WORTH LIVING

BY CRYSTAL SWANIGAN 165

Serve Well Thou Faithful Daughter By Rachanda Smith 176

"You Matter!" ~A Moment Between Lovers~
By Danielle Bennett 184

Power To Laugh By Dr. Clarice Howard 195

From The Valley To The Mountain Top (Soaring)
By Joyce Kamau 204

Unleash Your Destiny By Kelisha Worrell............................ 216

Catching Hell On Another Level Became My Blessing
By Dr. Jacquelyn Hadnot 226

Identity Crisis By Dr. Darline Nabbie 237

Born Leader, Designed By God By Tara Nicole Green 244

Re-Ignited To Walk In Power By Laila Miller 252

I Am The One By Shaquatta Edgar... 259

If Not You, Then Who? By Deidre A. Calcoate........................ 269

Leaders Lead By Sonia Merrit.. 279

The Power Of Saying Yes By Lakeisha Richards 285

Stepping Out Of The Shadows By Sandra Hale 296

My Emotional Trauma Almost Took Me Out
By Michelle Alston 306

Discover Your Limiting Beliefs And Strengthen Your
Relationships By Giselle Vazquez 316

Life Challenges... Just Stepping Stones Working For My Good
By Mary Davis... 325

WOMEN OF POWER: IGNITED TO SERVE

Foreword An Interview By Jaresha Moore

Hello, my name is Jaresha Moore. I had the honor of sitting down with the Visionaries for the Women of Power Ignited to Serve Anthology, Apostle Deborah Allen and Dr. Pamela Henkel, to learn more about their vision for the book you are now holding in your hands. Here is the account of how this interview with these two Powerful women went.

Jaresha: As visionaries of the Women of Power Ignited to Serve Anthology, tell us what Ignited to Serve means to you for your book collaboration and everyday life.

Apostle Deborah Allen: This Anthology is everything in this season of my life. I'm really just excited to think about the Anthology, Women of Power Ignited to Serve; it really shows the heart of the women in this book. It shows our hearts that we are women that are doing great things. We're moving in greatness, and yet we're moms, pastors, and wives, but we're also doing anthologies—so many things in this season of our lives. So, we get to see women on a different level, not just working but also serving. Our heart is to serve. Serve our families, serve our communities, and serve each other and our sisters. So, this Anthology will be impactful because you get all these women who are powerful in their own right. Yet, we are coming together to serve the needs of many people.

Dr. Pamela Henkel: Oh my gosh, Apostle, that is so beautiful, and I don't know what I could add to it. You know, we are all women in our own worlds with the things that are pulling on us. I mean, and today here, for the purpose of this interview, we are in different states, Jaresha, you're traveling; we all have other hats and are doing other things. I'm just going to let the cat out of the bag because we already did this interview once, and I, Dr. Pamela, didn't get the record button, so here we are doing it again.

You see, we are human, we are human beings, and human doings on the earth make a difference. We're not saying you have to be perfect. We're just saying you have to realize that there is a reason that you're here that is beyond the earthly realm. There's something that you're here to do. You can do that when we come together collectively. We can do something together that we could never do alone, which is under the umbrella of serving. Servant leadership, making a difference in the world.

Jaresha: Both of you are women of power, and you're truly movers, shakers, and influencers. What impact do you see Women of Power Ignited to Serve making in women's lives?

Apostle Deborah: I believe that we are a movement, and so does Dr. Pamela. I believe that this Anthology is going to shift so many lives on a global basis. Yes, we have women writing from other places, including Germany and Australia. I believe that we are global voices; that we are women called to change lives and to be impactful. We are women of power standing, and we are strong, but we are also women who serve, and we bring that to our families, our communities, and our businesses. So, we are women of power; we're strong, yet we're women.

I love that I can be great and still be a woman. I can have my own and still be a woman. I can make my own money and still be a woman. So, that is the beauty of Women of Power Ignited to Serve, we have strength, but we are gentle, kind, loving, and nurturing. In this season of our lives, we nurture and love the people around us and worldwide. The women are coming out to nurture and help it develop things.

Dr. Pamela: That is so true, Apostle. It's a global thing, and I see that there's going to be such a great increase in the influence of all of these women in this Anthology and they're going to grow in the stature of how much others are looking to them for guidance. If each of us just stops and takes a little pause – out of 34 authors, we all take a look around our little world, and we realize that we're influencing people in our little world. We are igniting them into their purpose. To have servant hearts, servant leadership in everything they do. If all of us are doing that, we're changing the world. We are making a difference. Better together making a difference, leaving that footprint on this planet. Talk about a legacy! You know we're not just leaving a legacy, Apostle; we are living the legacy!

Jaresha: That's so good. I love that, and it's so fitting. Because you just said that there are 34 authors, tell us more about your experience with being able to truly partner up and collaborate with other women of power.

Apostle Deborah: I believe it is our heartbeat. We have served women for decades. I would say that women have been our heartbeat for a long time, and we are women. We are God's women. This Anthology was not hard at all to put together. The sisterhood and the love Dr. Pamela and I have together, coming out of the Power Voice Summit together, being in the Thinking Into Results Program, and also being together in the Inner Circle with Jon Talarico, we work together well. That servanthood mind is there, and so is the mind of greatness in both of us. It has really allowed us to really fit hand in hand, where we can flow easily. Working together in this Anthology has been an easy process because we are so like-minded. We are both great in our own right, but we're better together.

That's the thing about this Anthology, I would say that you could be good in your own right, but together we are just so powerful as a group. We can conquer more things together than we can apart. That is the benefit of this Anthology, that all these women we have worked with in coaching, counseling, and ministry are coming along to ride with us to be a part of this great movement that we are doing in this Anthology.

Dr. Pamela: I love it, you're right! We have been in the vein of helping women as ministers and as leaders. We have been doing that, and we help men too, but very strongly dominating is a call to empower women. That's obvious when you put together an author call, and 32 women show up; that is saying something, isn't it? They're saying, "I will follow this leadership."

Apostle Paul said, "Follow me as I follow Christ," and it wasn't that he was trying to say, "Hey, be big and bad like me, I'm perfect." He was saying, "Follow my lead because the lead that I'm following is perfect."

So, to me, that's sort of the where it has been at with Apostle and I. As we are endeavoring to be like that saying, "Follow me as I follow after God and as I follow His leading." When He's directing me to do, and I do that to the best of my ability, He takes care of the rest of it. I do my ability, He does the rest with His, but we can then be that leadership for others.

It has been such a blessing, Apostle, to work with you because you are a woman of incredible power. I mean, like dynamite, she's amazing and so down to earth. There's no competition between her and I, and that is not always the case, not just with women but people in general. It's usually like everybody wants to compare; look at it as a battle. You know, Apostle and I have found, we don't have to compete with each other and say, "I got a better one than you." We don't have to do that. We just lead from our hearts and enjoy the position giving each other a boost. Saying, "Let me help you, step up," and then as we're doing that for one another, everybody around us is doing it for each other. That's where there's power, in unity.

Esther was Queen, right? But she wasn't brought to the palace just so she could wear a crown. She was brought to the palace so she could make a difference in the world. But, to make a difference in the world she had to go back to her support team and say PRAY. Everybody has their next, and it's so fun to see these women step into their next, and it's been just an honor to do this with Apostle at my side; she is just brilliant.

Jaresha: I know that you both have shared a little bit about your journey but could you please tell us more about your journey and what has led you to do this Anthology, Woman of Power Ignited to Serve?

Apostle Deborah: I love the fact that between Dr. Pamela and me, they get so many years in ministry together. We have over 50 years in ministry between the two of us. I am also like Dr. Pamela because we were servants young. I was called into ministry a long time ago. I have served the majority of my life in ministry; I had some teenage years where I strayed for about four or five years, then I got back on track. So, I've preached the gospel these last 30 years.

I am one of those people who it took 30 years for me to be anointed as a Bishop in the Pentecostal Apostolic Church. To be here named as a Bishop, a woman, and a woman of color to be a Bishop. Then I was affirmed as an Apostle, it was not an easy task, and neither was it for the faint-hearted. You have to have some strength to come in and get after it.

Even in ministry, we have to prove who we are. That's the key to being a woman; we are the only people who have to prove who we are, whether in ministry or business. But even there, you still have to keep the mindset of a servant so that you don't get caught up in competition. You can't let all those things sway you. You remember that you are here to serve. That's the great thing about this Anthology, we are women of power, we are ignited to serve, and it is who we are in our hearts.

Dr. Pamela: Yes, that's so true, and if each one of us is reaching the next one of us, then we get the job done. I mean, between Apostle and I, we have come on 60 years or maybe even a little more leadership experience. Some of that is ministry, and all of it is business. We've been there, and you know I like to give credit where credit and honor is due to those that have gone before us as women. Oh my gosh, you know my grandmother was a school teacher? Yes, a school teacher of history and home economics. I remember going to class with her, and she taught high school. I thought, "These kids are so big!" As I would sit at her desk and color in my coloring books. She was ahead of her time because she was not only a home economics teacher but also taught history. So, you're really stepping out there, you know. Those that went before us that plowed the ground for us, Apostle. To step in for us and run. I mean, when I stepped in and started running, I was told I was on fire for my purpose. I was on fire for my faith. Yet, where was I going? sI'm ready to run; I know I heard what I'm supposed to do. Then I'm being told to stop. What do you mean stop? I'm not gonna stop. You're ahead of your time. OK, great, then shouldn't I be steps ahead of you? I mean, really, that's what it came down to. So, I didn't stop. I just kept pushing.

As Apostle said, it was a fight, but it was worth it. There were times when I was hurt, there were times when I cried, and there were times when I almost gave up, but I didn't. I don't pat myself on the back and say, "Oh Pamela, you're so amazing," I say, "Oh God, you're so amazing!" The people that He positioned around me encouraged me not to give up and not quit.

Apostle, you and I had that baton handed to us, and we've run with it all this time. You have a different vein of people and areas of the of the country and the nation and even on the world and me in my area, vein and countries of the world. And now, together, we have merged, and now we are handing the baton to the next generations, but we're even sharing it all in ignited to serve. Each other's photons right here, let me ignite you… let me ignite you… let me ignite you, and we're encouraging these women to go, go, go! You can do it because we did it! It is just amazing to see what happens when you don't quit.

Who would have ever thought 25 years ago, Apostle, that you and I would be in this interview talking about changing the world as women and as leaders? That we would be the heads of ministries and businesses internationally? That we would be visionary authors, successful international bestselling authors, and that other women would be speaking to us for guidance? I stand in awe of it. It's only by the grace and by, of course, our willingness not to quit.

It's been a fun ride, but you're right, Apostle, there's a payday, and we're in one of those right now!

Jaresha: OK, I love that you said that you are passing the baton as well, as your goal is to continue to empower other women. What words of wisdom would you give the merging and future women of power who are on their own journey of being ignited to serve?

Apostle Deborah: Do not give up! It's easy to quit. Oh my gosh, the hardest thing I've ever had to do was to get back up again. That was one of the hardest battles I ever had to fight was to get back up again. So, I would tell the women, do not give up on you and bet on you. Let's just say that you got a bet on you, and that is so necessary because we see greatness in other people. Women give ourselves to everybody, but it's very important that we are women of power ignited to serve; even as we are serving, remember who you are, embrace it, and know that you will change the lives of so many people.

Dr. Pamela: If they don't give you a seat at the table, bring a chair! Yes, bring a chair. You know what you've been called to do, so if Apostle and I could press through and do all we did to get to where we are, you can too. One night when I was giving our little girl her bottle in the middle of the night, she's 13 now, so you know it was a while ago, but I was contemplating giving up. And, I know you've all been there. Maybe you're there right now. This epiphany moment happened when I really heard the voice of God speaking to me. This is what I heard, 'God's purpose never changes even if the plan does,' and that rocked my world. I was shocked to hear that. Wow, the plan had changed, but the purpose hadn't. What I felt called to do, and I had been doing and bumping up against this challenge and that challenge. It was right; that was not the plan I had, but God said His purposes do not change. So, if they don't have your seat at the table, bring a chair.

Jaresha: I just love that so much. If you had to give us just one word to describe the Woman of Power Ignited the Serve anthology, what would that one word be and why?

Apostle Deborah: FIERCE: Be fierce and stand. Life is a battle, and there are going to be many things that come against you, but you are built as women of power ignited to serve. We were born to win. I have to say it like my mentor and coach Les Brown, 'it is not over until we win,' and so you have to be able to be fierce. That means to endure, to stand, to be tough, and we are those women that are built to battle, but we are also built to serve. So, I have to throw the server hood in because it's not just the battling that we need, but we need women that can serve other people in humility, serve in love and give it to each other. This book is just so amazing because we have such great women on a global scale. We are here not just not to be strong, but we are here to show you our hearts. Ignited to serve the entire world because we were born for it.

Dr. Pamela: PURPOSE: Yes, our purpose is to serve, but we are also *ignited* to serve. It's not just, *may I bring you your shoes?* But in serving as servant leaders. And in serving all, we're changing the world. So we have a purpose, and we know it. We're ignited to run after it, change the world, and help somebody else get there and run with it. So, that fierce purpose, change the world fierce, purpose, ignited to serve. Yes, I love it, fierce purpose.

Jaresha: There are women all over the world that are both part of the Women of Power Ignited to Serve Anthology and those that will read the book. They will constantly be able to reach out and be a part of this journey with all of the amazing women. What message do you want to share with them as to why this Anthology will be life-changing?

Apostle Deborah: We have all these women that we hold hands within this Anthology. Our goal was to write, encourage, strengthen, and empower you. This Anthology is a global voice; we are women from everywhere, of all ages, stages, coaches, dreams, and young and middle-aged older women. All those women –even if my voice doesn't reach; even if Dr. Pamela's voice doesn't reach you, out of 34 authors, one of these women will reach you. You may need to be reinvented, you may need to get back up again, you need to be encouraged, you just may need some love, you may just need some strength, but out of one of us, I promise you our voice will reach you. That is why we came, to be the difference. The Women of Power Ignited to Serve – we came to change the world to understand that we were born for such a time as this and that our voices are needed on the earth for change.

Dr. Pamela: Yes, our voices are needed! You know, if reading this, if somebody would have told Apostle Deborah and I that we would be doing this – I don't know that we would have believed them. If somebody had said five years ago, I would have said, "That's exciting, but I don't have any idea how it's going to get done!"

A year ago, I would have said, "Well, that's really exciting. I'm excited about that, but I don't know. I think it's a little out of my league."

Let me tell you. YOU don't have to figure out how it's all going to happen. Just say, "yes," show up and say, "yes." Read this book, hear the stories, and see that the women within were there; they're just further down the road, maybe, but you could follow their lead. Get excited; your life matters and your story matters. You are here on purpose with a purpose by design and not by default. So, it's time to step into your greatness and take it to the next level.

Women of Power Ignited to Serve will be in your toolbox to carry on throughout the rest of your life.

Introduction
By Apostle Deborah Allen

Resounding in the air is the phenomenal boom of fierce destiny coming to fruition. Every woman of "POWER" in this anthology sounds the alarm that is clearly a clarion call of abundance, enlargement, service, and strength! Undoubtedly there is a fierce spark and activation for us to get back to the heart of the matter of why we do what we do. As I reflect and even ponder some things, I understand that a large part of me is just a plain servant. My heart is to assist others in living the lives of their dreams, and they were born to live. Unashamedly, I acknowledge the truth that women have been such a strong heartbeat of what I do and have done for over three decades. However, that's not just true for me but for every author in this dynamic anthology.

We are women that are on assignment and get things done even as we serve. We are powerful in our own right, yet we are all destined to be here together in this collaboration that's changing the world on a universal scale. Being servants comes from a fundamental place deep inside of us all. We each come from a place of courage, focus, loyalty, and wanting everyone to succeed. True servants think of others even when it's an inconvenience to themselves. Serving is so wowing and inspiring because you have to be a secure person and understand your call. Not only that, but servants must be selfless for others, which takes so much strength to achieve. Women Of Power "Ignited To Serve" has exploded as the global movement it was born to be. Relentlessly we are all seizing this opportunity to pour out into the lives of others!

Honestly, women are beyond magnificent creatures that are born to birth, lead, nurture and serve. It has been my joy, and the other author's joy to collaborate with women, celebrate women, and support & serve women. Not just women, but we have served families, communities, and the nation through the gifts and talents instilled in each of us. Finding one's inner voice can be a liberating, awe-inspiring, and transformational experience. Yet we must do it with the right heart and mindset. I incorporated the idea of sisterhood and camaraderie into this spectacular book. Also, the co-author's lives have been centered around helping women find, develop and birth their voices. I attest that women are at the heartbeat of a lot that I do and that I desire to see them be strong and fierce and know that they can truly achieve their dreams and walk in purpose. Society has forgotten the key to service and unity, but we have not hence the writing of this anthology. Collectively, we are here to help women come alive and recognize that serving is a powerful gift!

May the words of every fierce woman cause a fresh wind to stir up and rest upon you. May our words help you see that self-growth is necessary for finding, birthing, and embracing your purpose. When walking in purpose, fiercely walk in servanthood and divine authority.

Seriously, this book will be a tool that dares us to change our perceptions because they are what control the paradigms of our minds. It even determines how we see serving. We have teamed up to blow all expectations out of the water for this year with this anthology: Women Of Power "Ignited To Serve." Courageousness was needed even demanded when we all began this journey to write. Nevertheless, we dare you to shift, ignite, or serve on a greater level. Join us on this journey because this will be a pivotal moment in your life that will enlarge you. We are the ladies that are saying here we are, and Lord, send me! Understanding this anthology will water the dry places of your life. We are calling forward the women born to battle, serve, overcome and win. Refuse mediocrity on all fronts of your life. Now be the powerhouse that serves, excels, and ignites!

My motto:
"Let's fiercely ignite, rediscover, birth and unlock your purpose from within!"
Apostle Deborah Allen

About Deborah Allen

Finding one's *inner voice* can be a liberating, awe-inspiring, and transformational experience. Fashioned to help the masses find their "fierce"; is the dynamic professional, Deborah Allen.

Deborah Allen is a 4X international & 14X best-selling author, speaker, certified life coach, cleric, and CEO and creative founder of **The Fierce System**, a multifaceted liaison specialty, centered around helping women find and develop their voice.

Having been trained by world-renowned NSA motivational speaker, Mr. Les Brown, Deborah understands the importance of strategy, development, and credible mentorship, traits she seamlessly translates to her growing clientele.

Deborah's mantra is simple: Her only goal is to motivate clients, helping them create the life they were meant to live.

Refusing mediocrity on all fronts, Deborah has trailblazed a credible path for those she serves. She has served as Senior Pastor of Lighthouse Apostolic Ministries of God Church for the last 22 years; and is the Executive Director of the nonprofit organization, L.A.M. Ministries, Inc.

Matching servant leadership with incredible respect for higher learning, Deborah holds licenses as an RMA/CDA & Certified Life Coach. She is a member of the National Speaker Association Speaker (NSA) and a Black Speakers Network (BSN) Speaker. Her conglomerate, The Fierce System, is comprised of many platforms, including: Fierce TV, Radio, and blog, as well as the Fierce Voices of Destiny Program, where she mentors, develops and creates strategic alignment between clients, and their true life's calling.

Deborah proudly attests that women are at the heartbeat of all she does, and that it is her desire to see them be strong, fierce, and know, that they can truly achieve their dreams, and walk in purpose. When she is not out helping women to come alive, rebuild, shift and find themselves again; Deborah is a valued asset to her communal body, and a loving member of her family and friendship circles.

Deborah Allen. Energizer. Organizer. Servant Leader.

Deborah Allen ~ Contact Information

Links:
Facebook: https://www.facebook.com/deborahallenfierce
Instagram: https://www.instagram.com/deborahallenfierce/
Twitter: https://twitter.com/deborahallenfie

Periscope: https://www.pscp.tv/ladydeborahallen/follow

LinkedIn: https://www.linkedin.com/in/prophetessdeborahallen/

YouTube: https://www.youtube.com/channel/UCTOf0igcAxlVaneH2ZOo_Zg

1st Website: https://deborahallenfierce.com/

2nd Website: https://deborahallenspeaker.com/

The Fierce, Ignition & Activation Show/Podcast: https://envisionedbroadcasting.com/fierceignition%26activation?fbclid=IwAR03g_k7RO44QE1Ybahy2poVzktBDv08wX07e1X4N0yPF0Spi_MEataMG-o

Email: deborahallenfierce@gmail.com

Introduction
By Co-Visionary Author
Dr. Pamela Henkel

Did you know ....

Women make up 70% of the healthcare workforce globally and about **half** of all doctors.

They also make up 95% percent of all long-term care workers.

Even my Nation, the Good Ole USA, has a woman as Vice President. Women are arising everywhere ✦ Ignited To Serve!

It is an exciting time to be alive and to be female.

When Apostle Deborah Allen shared her amazing vision for this book, I was immediately **ignited to serve** this vision and run alongside her.

We are all here On Purpose with a Purpose by Design. I love empowering women to press into their Divine Purpose. The Ignited To Serve Anthology was a great way to do this on a global scale. Apostle Deborah lights the way when it comes to empowering women Fiercely into their greatness. Partnering with her in this endeavor has been life-changing. Every author is a Queen in her own right. These women are warriors Igniting Purpose, Passion, and Power everywhere they go. The vision of this book has been evident since its conception, "Women Go Change The World."

That vision is my vision.

To Your Greatness
BLESSINGS,
Dr. Pamela Henkel

DR. PAMELA HENKEL

About Dr. Pamela Henkel

Individuals seasoned with generous amounts of charisma, compassion, and undeniable essence, possess the kind of ingenuity; that shifts the world into its own greatness. Stewarding these traits in unyielding measure; is the spirited professional, Dr. Pamela Henkel.

Dr. Pamela Henkel is an International Best-Selling Author, multifaceted compere, speaker, elite coach, CEO, and Founder of both Purpose with Pamela and Pamela Henkel Ministries. Her multifaceted production and International radio conglomerate fashioned to enthuse women, entrepreneurs, authors, and diverse professionals to take hold of their life's purpose.

Dr. Pamela Henkel's mission is to add value to as many lives as possible. Reminding them that they are here on purpose with a Purpose by Design and not by default.

Partnering her passions with sincere regard for higher learning, community, and achievement. Dr. Pamela Henkel's career remains a reflection of creative grace, captivating the hearts and minds of many. She holds a doctorate in Philosophy, Christian Leadership, and Business. Living life as one dedicated to the service of people.

Hosting a myriad of professional skill sets without the compromise of her dedication to humanity, Dr. Henkel has maintained a nonpareil presence in the modern business world. As the creative founder of Purpose TV, The Pamela Show, and more, she extends her podcast, International radio, and social platforms to promote the voices of many on a global scale. Her propensity for success in her field has led her to award-winning achievements, such as the nomination as one of the Top 50 Women of Business, an elite membership of the Power Voice, as well as a personal mentorship from world-renowned speaker and mentor, Les Brown. Dr. Henkel's trusted expertise has yielded her various leadership positions, such as Client Enrichment Program Director at the Million in You Lifestyle, and Head Coach for the Inner Circle.

Dr. Pamela Henkel calls Minnesota home, where she is wife, mother, and grandmother to her loving family. As well as always encouraging people to be the salt and the light everywhere they go.

Dr. Pamela Henkel. Leader. Energizer. Philanthropist.
www.purposewithpamela.com
https://linktr.ee/Purposewithpamela

I Think I Can! (But Can I Really?)
By Dawn Lieck

Oh my goodness! The conversations we have with ourselves! Sometimes they aren't all friendly or positive, I'm sure we can all agree!

For as long as I can remember, I felt I was meant for so much more than where I was currently at. Whether it was my job or my personal relationships, I felt there was so much more for me. Note I used the word "felt" vs how I acted.

That little voice was steadily chatting in the back of my head. She would say things like; "You can do it Girl!" Then in the next breath she would say, "Well maybe you could if you knew how" or "You could if you were good enough to pull it off" "You could if you had enough experience like the others we see doing things" her chatting was absolutely endless! Whenever I felt strong and confident in a new plan, she would commence with her negativity until I put my plan back in the tiny box for which it seemed to live most of the time. I mean after all, she had some valid points. She had so many more reasons why I couldn't accomplish my goals, I couldn't beat her numbers with reasons why I could.

This is such a hard battle to win with ourselves. Brutal actually. It's much easier to concede than it is to fight to win!

This battle raged within me for many years. Miss Negative Nancy (as I call her) and her steady voice of mediocre expectations of me seemed to be my fate.

Here's what I learned to be true; her negative voice would definitely be the truth of my destiny, as long as I believed and accepted what she was telling me.

Our minds are so very powerful in every aspect of our lives. I had experienced great opportunities that had been lost or ruined by over thinking and listening to that endless chatter in my head.

I am a firm believer that God will take you exactly where he wants you to go, WHEN he wants you to go. I had been listening to that negative voice telling me I couldn't, I wasn't worthy and that everyone else was better than me for so long that I held it as my truth. So much so that I had deafened myself to hearing what God had been telling me all along. I was worthy, I was meant for more and I had a purpose.

As soon as I opened my heart, eyes and ears, my path was laid out for me. My success in business as well as my personal life began to flourish in miraculous ways!

When I look back at myself, I felt I had faith in God at the time, but in reality I had faltered in my faith. I had chosen to listen to my own negativity and fear instead of having faith in my Creator and knowing he had a purpose for me. It's not like I didn't know I was destined for more from the beginning. The fact is that I chose to believe otherwise. In doing so, I lived a life that was nowhere near happy or prosperous. There was always an emptiness within me. That emptiness was my lack of faith and obedience.

I've since learned to listen, pray on things, wait for my answer and when it's given, not let fear stop me from being obedient in the assignment. Having faith, conquering fear and staying obedient isn't always a flawless process on my part. The chatter still surfaces from time to time. The difference is that now I know how to quiet the negative chatter before it consumes my actions. I quiet Negative Nancy through prayer. I know all things are possible through Christ and being open to listen for his direction.

My business is growing in leaps and bounds. God has given me the man of my dreams 56 years into my life to grow old with. Everything I felt I could do I'm now doing through faith in God and my belief in myself. I have a completely different life now. Not only the one I wanted but the one I was meant to have from the beginning.

I will leave you with some thoughts to ponder. These three questions are a self-check and will give you the answer as to whether you are listening and if you really are, to whom?

1. What are the goals and dreams of your heart? (They were placed there.)
2. What's your plan of obedience to accomplish these things?
3. Are you walking in faith or listening to self-chatter?

Your choices will always be yours. Mediocre or Miraculous, choose wisely!

About Dawn Lieck

Dawn Lieck is a world-class business professional with remarkable expertise in the areas of business and multidimensional coaching.

A *mirrored portrait* of what it means to be a *"Renaissance Woman"*, Dawn's abilities have earned her professional respect amongst generational influencers.

Setting the standard in her field, Dawn is an International Speaker, best-selling author, and the CEO of both Finally Free, LLC, and Dawn Lieck

Enterprise. Affectionately known as the "Transformation Business Coach", Dawn helps successful professionals harness their true potential by putting them in touch with themselves on an intrinsic level. Having an unyielding passion for personal development, Dawn motivates clients to renew their perspective, conquer fear, and to create life balance using a system of pragmatic strategies.

Dawn's mantra is simple; "DO IT SCARED".

The result has been phenomenal, as Dawn has enjoyed wide-ranging success and is in high demand, from both domestic and international audiences. Dawn has held a three-year consecutive election, as one of the Top 100 Women to Know on the Gulf Coast, where she was also featured as a Woman of Achievement Entrepreneur Finalist.

Though her talents lead her reputation, her heart for service leads her path, as Dawn is involved in many organizations on the Gulf Coast including the Gulfport Chamber of Commerce Board, Back Bay Mission Advisory Council, Leadership Gulf Coast Graduate, VP Membership Chair for Lighthouse Business and Professional Women, Chair for Success Women's Conference and a team lead for women at Habitat for Humanity.

Email: Dawn@dawnlieckenterprise.com
Facebook: Dawn Lieck

Born to Serve
By Dr. Renee Huffman

The servant is the greatest of them all, according to Matthew 23:11. Being born and marked by God is not an easy task, but it's rewarding. When I was born, I had one fist full of obstacles, and my other fist was full of challenges. I was called, chosen, and commissioned by God to do a mighty work for the Kingdom of God at the age of seven years old. My service was to my parents first. My mother dealt with mental illness, and my father was told in elementary that he had a learning disability. This taught me how to serve at an early age, and I was determined by faith to win and be pleasing to the Highest God!

In the 8th grade, I became a Peer helper and within that same year I was elected to be a mediator amongst my peers. I learned how to listen to both arguments, while encouraging both sides to have an open mind to opposite viewpoints. My goal of uniting people together is a great quality to have and teach while serving people. Individuals want to know that your compassionate, and their story matters. Once you have listened and given a resolution, people tend to be grateful for your time and willingness to resolve the conflict with one another quickly.

At an early age, I was an advocate for my mother's mental health; I remember being 17 years old and going to my pastor and requesting for him and his wife to come to the hospital (mental health connected to the hospital) to pray with my mother, I was determined for her to get well. They went to the hospital, and my pastor and his wife prayed for my mother, and she recovered quickly. When I look back at this moment, I was walking like a servant.

According to the Merriam-webster dictionary, the word "servant" means one that performs duties about the person or home of a master or personal employer.

We are designed to serve, and we must learn from our greatest example Jesus Christ.

Matthew 25:36-40
English Standard Version
36) I was naked, and you clothed me, I was sick and you visited me, I was in prison, and you came to me.' 37 Then the righteous will answer him, saying, 'Lord, when did we see you hungry and feed you, or thirsty and give you drink? 38 And when did we see you a stranger and welcome you, or naked and clothe you? 39 And when did we see you sick or in prison and visit you?' 40 And the King will answer them, 'Truly, I say to you, as you did it to one of the least of these my brothers, you did it to me.'

In the summer of 2017, I was asked by a close friend to assist in serving the unfortunate and homeless in which I agreed to help. It was extremely overbearing and hot for us serving those in need with a majority requesting water. We begin the process by handing out water and facial wash clothes to begin a minimal cleansing. Still to this day the remembrance of one individual who stood out to me will never to be forgotten. My first encounter with this individual; he was sitting on the side of a building, and next to him was a man sleeping, positioned in his own vomit; at this moment, my life changed. A passion was ignited on the inside for me to serve and pour into the homeless. This gentleman began to experience the holy spirit once I began to talk; I could feel the presence of the Highest God, the gentleman requested me to be quiet, and the tears started to fall from his face, and God was performing a miracle right before my eyes. When you decide to serve God and His people, you must be an empty vessel and allow God to fill you with his love, compassion, and concern for the souls you encounter.

The second person I meant was a homeless young lady under a major highway, dead pigeons surrounded her, and she was the only female surrounded by men. I knew that this would not be an easy situation, but God had given me the heart to serve in difficult situations. I first asked for her first name only; most people never ask the homeless their name; they just refer to them as the homeless. It's so important to know them by their name because you acknowledge that they are human beings. I began to talk to this young lady; she had such a brilliant mind and had a background working in corporate America. The more we talked, the more I wanted to see her back on her feet and saved by the Highest God. To serve, you must be patient and go through the process to see a mighty change. My nonprofit, Dressed N Dignity, elected the young lady to be our first woman to go through our makeover process. I always tell people you can put lipstick on a pig, but it's still a pig; you must first work on the person inside before you makeover the outside.

My passion for the homeless ignited me to serve women like never before. Here's the background of Dressed N Dignity.

I had worked in Corporate America for almost 20 years. I remember during my senior year in high school (21 years ago), a non-profit organization by the name of Dress for Success came to my school campus to serve young women to transition from high school into the workforce; they showed us how to select proper suit attire and colors, hairstyles, and to implement necessary accessories to enhance our looks. I am forever grateful for Dress for Success for providing me with the necessary tools to be successful in my career. Fast forward 21 years later, a young lady was inquiring about clothing to wear for an interview, but the nearest location for clothing was 50 miles away. At that moment, I discovered there was a need in my local community, and I encompassed the tools to navigate and organize a non-profit to help women who need professional business attire, communication skills, resume building, interviewing tips, and business etiquette training. I decided to form Dressed N Dignity and place it within a 25-mile radius of any city within the Dallas-Ft Worth area to shorten the commute for women who are currently looking for employment.

Dressed N' Dignity is a nonprofit organization established in the fall of 2017. Our mission statement is to restore and empower women to walk in excellence in business, community, and family life by providing adequate business attire, communication skills, and necessary etiquette training.
Our vision statement is set forth to transform and enhance the lives of each woman as she becomes a mirror that reflects the next generation

Since the existence of Dresses N' Dignity, I'm extremely excited and proud to say we have professionally make-over multiple women and transformed their lives by planting seeds of hope. During the spring of each year, we have our annual women's business conference. "We also have a brunch during the winter season called Restore Her Dignity brunch. All events present dynamic local speakers of the community who help the women of dignity to strive and thrive on being all they can be. We also have a plethora of community women who are on top of their business entrepreneurship to sit at the tables during brunch to give advice and encouragement. These ladies, by my term, are called sister angels.

Now that I have been serving God for 20 + years, I serve in every area of my life. I own Women of Dignity Media, where we serve women in media from Women of Dignity Magazine to Women & Dignity Television. We have a charge from God to change the voice and the face of women in media. It's important to assist women in writing their narratives and telling how they have overcome so many challenges, different situations and have leaped over so many hurdles to become great. It's amazing how God will use you in different areas that many people believe that Christians should stay out of. But God desires for all people to be reached before he comes, and that's why I've been trained to be a servant of the Highest God! Our mission statement at Women of Dignity Magazine:

OUR MISSION

Women of Dignity Magazine focuses on telling the stories of incredible women who are impacting their local, national, and global communities. These women are CEOs of nonprofit organizations, ministries, corporations, authors, and small businesses.

By telling each woman's story, we hope to inspire the next generation and beyond to soar, strive, and succeed in life.

I will leave you with this my life quote: Stay In your lane or be disqualified. The meaning of this quote is to believe in yourself, and God will unveil the greatest that's on the inside, and you will have a great life of serving others.

My scripture: Galatians 5:13 KJV
For, brethren, ye have been called unto liberty; only use not liberty for an occasion of the flesh, but by love serve one another.

DR. RENEE HUFFMAN

About Dr. (HC) Renee Huffman

Dr. (HC) Renee Huffman is a number #1 Bestselling Author born and raised in San Diego, California, to Carl and Betty Jackson. Renee Huffman has over 18 plus years of proven experience in the Financial, Mortgage, Healthcare, and

Telecommunication Industries, where she has expertise in working with Fortune 500 companies such as AT&T, ING, BOEING, and ExxonMobil. Mrs. Huffman established Dressed N' Dignity as a nonprofit organization in the fall of 2017. Our mission statement is to restore and empower women to walk in excellence in business, community, and family life by providing adequate business attire, communication skills, and necessary etiquette training. In 2020 Renee became the owner and publisher of Women of Dignity Magazine, which focuses on telling the stories of incredible women impacting their local, national, and global communities. In 2021 Renee was appointed as a U.S. Delegate for Dubai connected with The Economic Hub. In February 2022 Renee Huffman was one of the Keynote speakers at The Leadership Experience @ the University of Michigan. In March 2022 Dr. Renee Huffman received an Honorary Degree of Doctor of Philosophy Christian Leadership and Business from Cornerstone Christian University in Atlanta, Ga.

FB Renee Huffman

FB Business Page: Women of Dignity Media

IG: DressedNDignity

Empowered to Serve
By Jaresha Moore

"There is no pain Jesus can't fill. There is no hurt that He cannot heal. All things work – according to the master's holy will." No matter what you're going through. Remember that God only wants a chance to use you. For the battle is not yours, it's the Lords."
(Lyrics, by Yolanda Adams; Battle is Not Yours)

The first time I heard this song, it sent chills through my body because I understood the words, but I felt the words and not just once but repeatedly. I had felt pain, hurt, disappointment, and tiredness and was taught as a child that God will never leave you nor forsake you. Yet, I knew that I would have troubles and face adversities. In those moments, we must call on HIM and understand that this battle is not ours; it's the Lords. Many women struggle with so many different things in our lives, such as anxiety, depression, hurt, pain, loss, disappointments, and the list goes on and on. I was one of those people who struggled with all the above as a single mom of 4, wanting more for my children and praying for God's blessing on our life. From financial hardship to experiencing a failed marriage, the only thing I knew to do was pray and praise. I would pray and ask God to order my steps and help me to discover and walk in my purpose so that I could help others. Praying for God to deliver me from brokenness and bondage to breakthrough and breakout, I knew God would provide if I could just keep pushing forward. I knew I wanted to empower others to recognize the greatness within that God helped me to realize in myself, and so my journey began.

Too Whom Much Is Given Much Is Required

The instrumental track started playing, and I started singing. It was my first time singing a solo at church, and I was nervous, but I knew that God would help ease my nerves once I started singing. I prayed with all eyes watching me from the congregation. It was as though they were anticipating that I had a testimony and God would allow me this gift. So, I sang and let the holy spirit lead me. It was emotionally for me because as I sang the words, I felt the words speaking and ministering to me as though I was the one listening and not singing.

"You are holy, Oh so Holy, You are worthy, Oh so worthy, You are faithful, ... what a privilege and honor to worship at your throne, to be called into your presence as your own."
(Lisa McClendon, You Are Holy)

As I finished the song and looked around, everyone was emotionally filled up, not because of me but because of God and the Holy Spirit. When you recognize who you are and whose you are, it's such an honor and privilege to be in God's presence and do His work. It's an honor and a privilege to serve as God's child.

That day changed my life because I learned an important lesson about life and God's purpose for my life. I knew that "to whom much is given, much is required." (Luke 12:48) God allowed me to use one of the gifts He blessed me with to minister to others. Before this day, I understood how God could use people but never imagined that he could use me as a single mom to minister to others. I believe It was through God's grace that, years prior, I experienced a health scare that had both the doctors and myself puzzled as to what was going on with me.

After giving birth to my son, I was hospitalized, and I thought I would never see my family or children again. But God stepped in and turned it around to not only healed me, but he put me in other people's lives to share my story to help them. Through God's grace, I knew that my story as a single mom of four didn't end with me going through pain, divorce, and disappointment. I knew that God had more in store for me, but I had to have faith, do my part, and not be so quick to throw in the towel. Yes, it was hard, and there were times when I cried out, "Lord, help me."

When I was pregnant and putting myself through graduate school, I was ready to stop, but God kept me focused on my why – my children. When I was in graduate school, I fought for a better life for my children and our legacy. A legacy that started with whispering a prayer as a little girl to help me so I could help someone else, not knowing that God would turn that prayer into bigger and greater things. And that prayer got bolder over the years, for the Lord helped me to empower others for growth and success. Lord, provide me with the tools and resources to empower the world. Consequently, I recognized that day I sang that song that God had a bigger plan, and the same way I was serving and ministering through song – God could use me, a single mom who was broken, to help the world in many different capacities.

It's Not About You!

The day I joined over 17,000 leaders in the John Maxwell Team, which is now called Maxwell Leadership, I was determined to add value and let God lead me so I could serve. Then, I didn't realize that God opens doors for us to lead and serve others, and more often than not, those doors were being built years prior. I didn't realize that my passion of wanting to empower others would position me for ministering on stages, on international radio, and on podcast platforms. God had a plan for me, and although I didn't know the doors that he would open, he made sure that I learned those important lessons that would help me be a better servant on my journey. He made sure I was equipped to empower.

Often, we don't take the time to see just how each puzzle piece fits into our life and journey. When I decided to step into my purpose and calling, it was through reflection that I saw just how amazing God is and how he designed each piece to fit perfectly. Even those puzzle pieces of failure, disappointment, and pain were designed with a purpose. I often reflect and think, what if I never experienced that storm in my life, and I am reminded that it was all necessary as God was preparing me for what was next.

I stepped into another world of serving others through the John Maxwell Team. It came with many challenges and obstacles, but God knew there was more coming. And then, one day, I got a phone call and an email asking me to speak for a corporate Women's Conference to over 1000 women about empowerment. My initial reaction was nervousness, self-doubt, and fear, and then I said a prayer for God to help me recognize it was not about me and to help me deal with me. God revealed that and so much more.

When you pray and ask God to help you empower others for growth and success, you must be ready for all the blessings and doors that God opens. That day, God opened the door for me to share my story with women and help them grow, but I first had to be willing to get out of my own way and let go and let God. Through my connection with Maxwell

Leadership, God revealed another important lesson that we often forget it's not about me. Sometimes, we need to remind ourselves that our purpose and how God calls us to Empower others is not about self. A quote says, "your gifts are not about you. Leadership is not about you. Your purpose is not about you. A life of significance is about serving those who need your gifts, leadership, and purpose."

When I spoke and poured into all those women, I knew that this was God telling me," It's not about you," and it's so much bigger and greater.

Empowered To Serve

Michelle Obama once said, "there is no limit to what we as women can accomplish." As women, we don't recognize the power that we have within us, and it's through our journey of storms, obstacles, pain, love, disappointments, and joy, God shows us our strength and resilience. Over the last 35 years, God has allowed me to experience opportunities to equip, encourage and empower others in so many different capacities with one purpose that started with whispering a prayer to help me help others. I am a living testimony of how God answered my prayer to walk into purpose, and he made provisions repeatedly for me to do just that.

In 2019, I had an opportunity to connect with someone in the media industry who shared information with me that would later impact the lives of thousands and thousands of people worldwide.

This opportunity was not only an answer to a prayer that a little girl whispered a long time ago, but it provided a platform for countless women to share their messages, testimonies, and stories with the world. When I think back on the day that I said yes to launching Envisioned Broadcasting, an international radio, and podcast network, only God knew what was coming. He knew back when I prayed as a little girl to help me help others at a time when I was being bullied and wanted to help other girls and kids not get bullied at school. God knew that it was bigger and greater than I could ever imagine. And, so he started putting the puzzle pieces together so that platforms would be created to empower others all over the world.

Today, I give God the Glory, Honor, and Praise for providing the resources, tools, and strength to use a single mom, who society often looks down on, to help empower others for growth and success.

About Jaresha Moore Smith

Jaresha Moore Smith, MBA is the Founder/CEO of Empower On Purpose, LLC, where we provide leadership training and personal and professional development coaching and consulting services; Executive Director and Certified Coach, Speaker and Trainer for the John Maxwell Team, best-selling author, success and empowerment coach with over 18 years of combined experience in Education, Finance, Healthcare, and Business Management and Development and Sales; Owner of Envisioned Broadcasting Radio Station and host of Empower Hour with Jaresha. Envisioned Broadcasting is the station that equips, encourages, and empowers others for growth and success.

Born and raised in Dayton, Ohio, Jaresha 's passion lies in motivating, inspiring, and empowering emerging leaders, entrepreneurs, and business professionals to develop their leadership skills and businesses. As a single mother of four, Jaresha identifies with the challenges one faces with adversity, fears, self-doubt, and the many obstacles that life tends to send our way. As a result, she has used her experiences and training to build a successful brand, business, and legacy for her children. Jaresha believes that when life gives us lemons, that is a way to make lemonade and turn it into an opportunity to use that lemon to teach and empower others.

Jaresha is a member of (WiBN) Women in Business Network, (NAPW) National Association of Professional Women, (ACHE) American College of Healthcare Executives, and (POWER) Professional Organization of Women of Excellence Recognized and an active Board Member of Human Race Theatre Company.

Embracing Our Strengths
by Jodie Solberg

As you grow older, you will discover that you have two hands; one to help yourself and another to help others.
-Audrey Hepburn

I spend my days helping women heal. Women who have been told for years, sometimes their whole lives, that what they think, believe, and are talented at doesn't matter. They need to dim their light, play small, be quiet, and not bother anyone by being their true selves. These women don't acknowledge their unique strengths, gifts, and abilities because they don't know what they are anymore. They have pushed down the parts of them that make them special and individual for so long that it's gotten lost deep within. My greatest gift is to be their guide in rediscovering who they were truly meant to be. This is my story of discovering and harnessing that power. In sharing my experience, my hope is that you will learn ways that you can do the same.

Growing up, I was encouraged to be independent, find my own way, and explore my personal interests. I had a strong sense of justice and fairness, strong beliefs and opinions, stood up for others, and understood their pain. Even from a very young age, I was highly empathic. People opened up to me as they felt my calming energy and that I would be a safe space to share their innermost thoughts and feelings. Because of this natural gift, I was even asked to counsel my peers in high school when a fellow student passed away in a tragic accident. These early experiences shaped who I have become and how I have chosen to serve others positively, but the flip side is that when I was younger, I was also highly emotional. I cried easily and often as I felt others' emotions intensely. I often felt what people were going to say before they said it or even without them saying it at all, and I understood the unspoken trauma they were dealing with. When another child got hurt, I cried as if it were happening to me. I just didn't know how to manage that yet, to separate my own feelings from those of others.

In addition to being empathic, I am also naturally curious, with a strong desire to learn all about how people live, what they think and believe, and why. This led me naturally to a career in the mental health field. Since managing emotions is such a pivotal part of any mental health professional's daily life, it was crucial for me to learn how to create and enforce boundaries, managing my own energy and emotions in a healthy way. Doing so has made the experience of being an empath positive, peaceful, and rewarding, rather than feeling burdensome and exhausting. I also learned how to be assertive and to model emotional strength and resilience for my clients. It has greatly improved my personal relationships and taught me that I need to take care of myself first to serve others with strength. Because I acknowledge empathy as a blessing, not a curse, I can guide others in tapping into their inner strengths, expressing their emotions, identifying the root cause of their challenges, and helping them heal and find ways to move forward.

While I have embraced my empathic nature as my greatest strength, many people's natural abilities go unrecognized. If we don't learn to harness our strengths, they can mistakenly be perceived as weaknesses. Often people don't recognize strengths within themselves because they just don't know how to use them or build them up so that they will serve both themselves and others. When you nurture your strengths, you can build them up to become your very own superpowers. Doing so will allow you to fulfill whatever your own life's purpose truly is. Here are more of my top personal strengths and how I have learned to harness them and step into my power so that you can see how I use them to serve others.

The next strength that was evident in my childhood was inclusion. Since birth, being an introvert, I may have been quiet and reserved but I have also made friends easily throughout my life with all different groups of people. As a child, I was very shy with new people, but I also invited others to play and be a part of the group as it pained me to see anyone left out. In high school, rather than always sitting with one group at lunch, I had friends in all the different crowds and backgrounds, and it was universally accepted because of my genuine caring for others. My strong sense of fairness meant that everyone around me knew I would stand up for them whenever needed. Now, in my mental wellness practice, this strength gives the clients I serve comfort and security knowing that our work together is a safe space where they can share their innermost thoughts and feelings with someone neutral, inclusive, and free from judgment.

Another of my strengths is my love of learning. I have always been an avid reader, and I enjoy the process of expanding my knowledge and understanding of people and learning how to serve them in deeper and more meaningful ways. Along with that comes my strength in problem-solving. I have a strategic mind that allows me to see behavior and thought patterns and be mentally prepared for multiple outcomes. In learning more about my clients, I clearly see their strengths and the ways they can overcome or avoid potential obstacles, which helps me guide them in their journey. I support them in reflecting, creating a clear vision, and thinking ahead about the potential results taking a particular action or path may have. In sharing my strengths of learning and strategy with others, they are better equipped to help themselves.

The last two strengths I recognize from childhood are my self-assuredness and sense of responsibility to serve others. Growing up, I had my own unique perspective based on personal experience and observation, in addition to what I learned in school and what was modeled for me at home. I needed to figure it out on my own, trust my inner voice and do what was right for me as an individual. I may have been quiet, but I always had strong inner confidence in my values, beliefs, and judgment. Starting my career, I had to develop and project outward confidence as I began supervising visitation, parenting coaching, counseling children and teens, and working with clients battling abuse and addiction. It also meant drawing on my strength of responsibility by exhibiting dependability, being a woman of my word, and honoring my commitments. This is an important strength in working therapeutically because my clients need to know that they can count on me to be stable and reliable.

As my career progressed, I was doing the work serving others to fulfill my purpose, but I was challenged in clearly defining my vision of who and how I could serve them best. I had difficulty managing my time and energy, and I overworked myself to the point of exhaustion and ultimately chronic burnout. I was aware of my special talents and skills in helping others heal, but I spread myself too thin and didn't prioritize my self-care. Building my private practice and customizing it to my strengths, putting systems in place to guard and protect my energy, and having greater work-life harmony have allowed me to serve others in a more profound and meaningful way.

When doing this work of personal discovery and growth, it's not always easy to think of good things about yourself. Have you ever sat in an interview dreading the question, "What are your strengths?" If so, you're not alone. Melinda Gates once said, "A woman with a voice is, by definition, a strong woman." It's time to find your unique voice, so you can own your power and embrace, develop, and harness your unique strengths, and allow them to ignite you to serve others as your best self. Most strengths are not skills that can be learned; they are innate, so the first step to finding your strengths is to look at what you do well and what others have praised you for in the past. We are all created with unique and powerful gifts and abilities that come so naturally that we often don't even recognize them because it feels so normal to us. We don't understand that what is second nature to us may be something another person has to work hard at, or that others simply don't possess. These are things we are born with, so these are signs of our strengths very early on. Looking back at childhood, how did you interact with the world around you? What did you want to be when you grew up? What is it about those things that drew you to them? What brought you joy then and now? What are you naturally passionate about, and who do you love serving? The common denominators, motivating factors, and deeper meanings behind the answers are where you may find your hidden strengths.

Since it can be difficult to see our own positive traits, you can also ask others who know you well what they think your strengths are. Another option is to take a strengths test online to uncover your top strengths. Once you figure out what your strengths are, you can begin to see all the ways they have shown up in your life. Keep in mind that the purpose of doing this is to increase your awareness of your strengths to build them up, not to compare them to others wishing you were different. Theodore Roosevelt once stated, "Comparison is the thief of joy." Being aware of our strengths helps us know how we can best serve others while also showing us who to surround ourselves with that can complement our strengths with their own. Don't fall into the trap of seeing those things that aren't your strengths as weaknesses or faults. They may be viewed as potential areas of growth or simply things to be aware of, but otherwise, it's best to release them all together and allow others to shine who have those as strengths themselves. We spend too much time trying to be who we aren't, perhaps what we perceive others want us to be, and fighting against our true nature rather than working with it. Finding what makes you unique is what will guide you to your purpose, fuel your passions, and show you the path to follow in serving others.

Once you've discovered your own top strengths, it's time to recognize yourself and then develop and harness them. Look at how you can better incorporate your strengths into your personal life, your work, and in how you are best able to serve others. When you build your life around doing what you are best at, you will find more peace, joy, fulfillment, and harmony. Trust yourself by tapping into your inner wisdom and listening to your intuition. Being more in tune with your inner voice will allow you to be more in flow with who you are and will guide you in making decisions. It's time to find the courage to live your life as authentically you. To create your own definition of who you are, what you want, and what success and happiness mean. Everything we do is in service to others, whether you work with people directly or not. Growing your strengths will allow you to give your best YOU to the world and share your unique and powerful voice. You will only truly be able to love and accept yourself, own your power, and serve others as your highest self when you embrace your strengths.

About Jodie Solberg

Jodie Solberg is a Mental Wellness and Success Coach, Certified Master Hypnotherapist, and International Best-Selling Author. Jodie loves working with purpose-driven professional women on a mission to live in alignment with their passion and values to create real and lasting change in their lives and the world around them. She helps them tap into the power of their subconscious mind to gain the clarity and confidence they need to up-level and achieve both their personal and professional goals.

Jodie has been working therapeutically for more than 20 years, with degrees in both Psychology and Sociology. She started her entrepreneurial journey as a consultant and coach for female entrepreneurs while still in graduate school studying Clinical Psychology, which is where she first began practicing as a Hypnotherapist as well. Jodie's experience working with diverse populations such as women and children suffering from the effects of abuse, teens in after school programs and group homes, parents in training programs, people dealing with chronic illnesses and addiction, and burned-out caregivers gives her a unique perspective to help her clients overcome their limiting beliefs, break through blocks to progress, and heal past hurts so they can be free from anxiety and fear, beat burnout, and have more peace, joy, and harmony in their personal and professional lives.

Alongside her therapeutic work, Jodie is known for her work as a consultant and coach for women in business. Her transformative coaching programs build self-esteem and confidence and increase her clients' focus, strength, resilience, and emotional intelligence. She also teaches about the importance of prioritizing self-care so they can go out and give back to their families and communities to create positive changes in the world and serve others as their best selves.

Jodie founded Psyched Up Success in 2019, fulfilling her long-standing dream of having her own private mental wellness practice working virtually with clients worldwide. Jodie's greatest joy and purpose is in helping other women to find their voice, become their best selves, create a life they love, and pass those lessons on to the next generation of strong, independent women. In addition to her professional fulfillment, she is a great contributor to her community with a long history of volunteerism. Jodie has always been a believer in creating work-life harmony, so she enjoys spending time outdoors and traveling with her family in search of great food, music, and culture.

To connect with Jodie, please email her directly at jodie@psychedupsuccess.com or visit her website at www.psychedupsuccess.com You may also follow her on social media on Instagram at @psyched_up_success or Facebook at @psychedupsuccess

The Emancipation Of Shame
By Angela Bennett

Secrets have a cost. They have a benefit too, and therein lies the rub. I had kept my secret for so long because the benefit was my dignity, reputation, and sense of self in the world. None of those things coincided with being a high-class prostitute. My boyfriends were not met conventionally. The 'how did you two meet' stories were always concocted, fabricated, and manufactured. That's what secrets do… they force you into a new lineage of falsehoods, which all have relatives and generations of new lies stemming from them, to keep them in line, in check.

I thought the cost was worth the benefit. I also thought I was in control.

It was, after all, my secret to tell.

Until it wasn't…

And the man in question was my client. Someone with whom I had shared intimate details and who I thought I could trust because of our circumstances… because I knew he too, could keep a secret.

Until he couldn't, or wouldn't.

At the time, I was preparing to leave the man I had called my love for three years. My sturdy, paramilitary trained, gym obsessed, Muscle Man of a partner. The relationship had soured beyond my ability to keep it, and signs of the end had been a long time coming. I hid many things from him, but none so big as the secret of what I did for extra money.

Everything I had shared with my client was about to be made public and used against me. And I was about to pay dearly. My client had turned my stalker and, in his obsession, took it upon himself to track down and tell my secret to my Muscle Man.

The fallout was devastating.

Alone, asleep in bed after my Muscle Man found out, he came into our bedroom and, before I even realised he was in the room, he had his hands wrapped tightly around my throat. He was a man who knew how to kill, and he was strangling me to death. The moment before I was about to pass out, I prayed to God and heard a message to look him in the eyes and plead for my life, which I did.

By some miracle, my Muscle Man released me. I gasped and jumped out of bed, but he caught hold of me on the run. He picked me up like a rag doll and threw me across the room, seething in disgust about what he had learned about me. You don't forget the look in the eyes of someone so mad they sought to end your life. The memory is seared in my brain forever, but I have learnt that your life can end in many ways.

My Muscle Man proceeded to contact everyone I knew and reveal my secret. To out me so wholly and vilely to everyone I loved. To my father, my siblings, my friends, and worst of all, my children. He did not even spare my children, which felt like an ending I would not live through. Like my stalker, he aimed to destroy my life and every relationship I had ever built, nurtured, or cared about.

The control I thought I had all along over my secret was a farce from the beginning. I was exposed on a whim, a crazy, jealous impulse, and then almost killed on another. Everything I had spent years covering over was laid bare for the world to see in the cruellest fashion. I had no control over what was being disclosed and discussed with everyone I had ever known. I had no control over the story, no ability to spin it my way, flavour it with empathy, or bake in some sympathy. It was raw, unadulterated, and told from a boiling and zealous male perspective.

Every stereotype of sordid was piled upon me, and I had no idea who I could trust or where I could run to feel safe. Most people turned their back on me in condemnation, but those who didn't will always be the ones who didn't. My best friend did what true best friends do; my sister and a few of my brothers stood beside me as my whole world crumbled – as all my secrets were exposed.

Terrified for my life and my children's lives, I spent the next year in hiding. I changed my name, closed down all social media accounts, and spent every day of those twelve months looking over my shoulder everywhere I went.

The secret had come out so maliciously that it had not only tainted my past, it felt like a past I could never outrun. The tentacles of guilt and shame were long, and their claws held me captive. Everything I did, I felt their grip tighter around me and the thought of any kind of future for myself or my children, when my past was so mired in shame, was hopeless.

How could I ever show my face again? Anywhere. The burden was overwhelming. That year was a horror, but in time I started to feel that enough was enough. There was only so much pain I could take responsibility for. I had had enough of hiding, enough of enduring menacing and threatening emails from the two men who had forced me down this path, and enough of allowing anyone else to have control over the reins of my life.

I decided to no longer permit them to be the masters over my past and my future and lay claim over so much of my life. The mistakes were mine, the choices were mine, and the past was mine, not theirs.

So too was the future going to be all mine. These two men had rendered me powerless for long enough, and it was my time to take back control of my story and my life.

Yes, they had exposed me, but no, they had not destroyed me. If anyone was going to do that, it was me! And if anyone was NOT going to allow that to happen, it would also have to be me. Yes, they had already released their version of my story, but I still had my version to release. It was not the impetus I would have wanted, but it was the cards I was dealing with, and so I made another decision to start again, using my own secrets as my secret weapon. To use them, as my truth, my story to empower and liberate myself from the weight of them. To bring my story into the light and see if anyone else could use it to liberate themselves.

I knew that everyone makes mistakes, and we are not meant to have to pay for them over and over. I wanted my truth to be in the world, in the cold light of day, so that I could be free to be myself and live into my future as a woman with a past she had not only lived through but learned from and triumphed over.

They say that "the truth will set you free," and for me, it did in many ways. I also want my truth to be a vehicle of permission for others to say what they have kept secret, often for years, if not decades. There is an old African proverb that resonated with me as I was finding my feet to speak my truth, and it says:

"... if there is no enemy within, the enemy outside can do us no harm..."

I had to learn the depth and the truth of this in my own way. Everyone does.

The irony was that the enemy who had tried to break me, ended up liberating me. Now, that took time to reconcile, but the domino effect was that my stalker's exposure of my secrets unleashed me. He unveiled me, and yes, it took the pain of looking into the darkness of my own shadows, but I eventually recognized my own power in it all. That I did not have to be ashamed or afraid of my past, that if I could take responsibility for it, I could have full authority over it.

And forgiveness.
And acceptance...

I could accept who I was, what it was, and I could accept who I am now. And I would know the difference between the two. And I do. I am proud to acknowledge that I am no longer in a position where I am being mastered by my past, which is exactly how the enemy operates. I have faith in who I am, who I have had to become, and I have faith in my future, not in spite of my past but because of it.

You intended to harm me, but God intended it for good to accomplish what is now being done, the saving of many lives. Genesis 50:20 NIV

Along the way, I have also had to carefully pick apart what I did against who I am. There are many reasons people do things, yet it is often not reflective of who they are as a person. A mother might steal for her child but not consider herself a thief. Even when it is not a dire one, a need can lead us to decisions that are against our grain, our character. Most people will never understand my reasons, but I have learned that they do not need to.

I just needed to know that, for me, it was out of character. Out of alignment with who I was. Even as I did the work, I knew I was not my full self. I was not condoning what I was doing to myself, and so I no longer attach my identity to it. I own it as part of my story, of what I did, but not as who I am.

Part of why I kept my secret was because of the judgment of others, the accusations I feared and loathed, but even that rationale gave all my power away. Yes, there may be reasons to be discreet, but for me, personally, I hid it from everyone in my life that I loved, and that was the price I then paid—the shame of the lie and the cover up and the years spent in that spin cycle.

I may have had an actual stalker, but we all have a saboteur in our midst.
Namely, our thoughts. Our mind can be just as dangerous. We all have thoughts of doubt and insecurity, fear and shame from things in our past that stalk us and keep us up at night, that lurk in the background of our psyche every time we dare take a step forward. Thoughts of unworthiness that hold us back forever.

Unless we decide to change and serve those thoughts with notice that things are changing, discern that your higher self is aware that your ego and these thoughts are trying to keep you under their power and control, and notice that it stops today.

You never lost your worth, even when you lost your way, and you are taking your power back over your mind and actions. No matter what we do to avoid it, our past has a way of running us down, so let it. Let it form part of the matrix of who you have become.

The truth of my own story is that I invested so much energy in keeping my secret a secret for so long that when it was betrayed, I had no way of knowing that the outing of my secret would reveal itself, in time, to be the only door to my liberation and the express lane to helping me change my life and harness a desire to share my blemished story to help others share theirs. The shame of my secret surfacing became the visibility of me, in all my wholeness, and the permission piece for others to live beyond the shame of any secret they hold within.

It was a long road but a worthwhile one, in which a great service was offered me by outing the shame in me. The only freedom we can truly feel in life is when we unshackle ourselves from our inner secrets, and my aim is to be an example to others, men and women, that it is possible to liberate ourselves through the emancipation of our shame.

About Angie Bennett

The transformative power of personal restoration, self-actualization, and radical change; is often fueled by anomalous individuals who've mastered their own personal storms to act as a reliable anchor in the lives of others. Proving this ethic undoubtedly; is the effervescent world-changer, Angela Bennett.

Angela Bennett is an author, coach, and CEO, and **founder of Angie B Transformation's;** a multi-dimensional coaching specialty, centered on the complete revitalization of the lives of broken women. Seamlessly infusing personal style assessment and recreation, coupled with the facilitation of transformative life coaching, Angela offers clients an authentic depiction of what life looks like when changed by the power of spiritual, physical, and mental edification.

Her mantra is simple: As one reshaped from the ashes of an unfortunate past, Angela exists to help women know and understand that one's past does not define them; it refines them. She pledges to reach out to those who are at their personal breaking points; lifting them out of the pits they find themselves in, as she has done, for herself.

Proving her skill sets uniquely quintessential, Angela Bennett displays a sincere regard for professional accretion, education, and personal achievement. She is certified in a myriad of vocations, including personal styling, Clean Health 1&2, Transformational Coaching Mastery, and much more. Polarizing audiences with her transparent and energetic orations, Angela is the proud mentee of World-Renowned speaker and coach, Les Brown; and has completed and facilitated several public speaking workshops and intensives, under his tutelage.

Inspired by the will to see lives transformed, Angela remains as one driven by the diligence of ethics, life composition, and the essence of personal renewal, in the lives of other women.

When Angela is not out changing the world for the better, she is an asset to her local communal body, and a loving member of her family and friendship circles.

**Angela Bennett. Leader. Motivator. Advocate.
Contact Angela (Angie B) on
<https://linktr.ee/angieb_transformations>**

Hope Against Hope: Green Light Grace
By Shervondaline S. Breedlove

Our bright June morning started wonderfully! I was so excited to be in a new state and looking forward to countless new beginnings. Jayla was dressed in a beautiful shade of yellow from head to toe for her first doctor's appointment in Mississippi. She received several compliments from the staff as we were welcomed into the new office. Dr. Wilson was very soft-spoken, thorough, and knowledgeable. I felt so good about her attention to detail and feedback during Jayla's examination. All seemed to be going well. The doctor and nurse stepped out of the room when Jayla's check-up concluded. After a few minutes, the nurse returned to calmly inform me that I needed to take my precious new infant to the children's hospital directly across the street immediately.

In a matter of seconds, my sunny disposition and optimistic outlook, which perfectly matched Jayla's outfit, quickly shifted to feeling startled and overwhelmed. As soon as we arrived, the hospital staff grabbed my sweet baby and rushed away in the opposite direction. Then a massive set of metal doors slammed behind them. Instant panic, anxiety, dizziness, numbness, shock, trembling, and uncontrollable tears hit me all at once. I told my mom, "They are going to slice my baby's tiny head open!" She shrilled, "Oh my God, Shervon, do not say it like that!" while we were waiting in the hallway for Jayla's hospital room to be assigned. The nurses brought a gurney into the hallway because it appeared that I was going to faint.

A neurology care coordinator came into her hospital room about an hour later. I was still in a daze. So, I watched her lips moving, but I was not comprehending any of the words she said. She proceeded to hand me a stack of books about Hydrocephalus, AV/VP shunts, operation details, and recovery. As a formality, I said, "Thank you.", as I thought to myself, "Ma'am, I could not read one word in these books - even if you gave me a million dollars right now!" At times, I still shudder when I think about the broad range of emotions I felt in those four thousand four hundred and forty minutes.

Jayla's brand-new pediatrician cared enough to come and check on her that evening after clinic ended in her office. She explained that she knew Jayla needed the critical procedure because she observed significant symptoms that confirmed her diagnosis. She assured us that Jayla was in the best hands with her new world-renowned neurosurgeon. Unfortunately, although he was a spectacular brain specialist, his bedside manner was not his best that day. He spoke very bluntly about Jayla's recovery and future prognosis during our conversation. "We will have to just wait and see how her body responds to the device. Since she is so young, she might not ever walk, talk, grow, or do anything." I listened to every word he said, but I did not accept them.

I began pleading The Blood of Jesus and speaking The Word of God over her life. I remembered that Abraham staggered not at God's promises to him. That is the type of tenacious faith I knew I had to develop and maintain throughout our journey. Parenting a child with Special Needs requires praying, fasting, and believing on a whole new level. Hope in God becomes your lifeline.

"Even when there was no reason for hope, Abraham kept hoping - believing that he would become the father of many nations. And Abraham's faith did not weaken. At about 100 years of age, he figured his body and Sarah's womb were both good as dead. Abraham never wavered in believing God's promise. In fact, his faith grew stronger, and in this, he brought glory to God. He was fully convinced that God is able to do whatever he promises. And because of Abraham's faith, God counted him as righteous."
{Romans 4:18-22 NLT}

Enduring so many helpless times gave me plenty of reasons to lose hope. However, just like Abraham,

I continued to believe what God's Word said. I adopted Abraham's "stagger not" mentality. I repeatedly spoke these words, "Jayla *will* walk, talk, grow, and live to declare the works of The Lord." {Psalm 118:17}

Jayla's first operation was a success. Her recovery was uneventful, and she was developing normally. My family was so proud of Jayla's progress. She was a happy baby and met the targets for each of her milestones. I purchased all Christian and educational toys, books, music, and videos for her. I was determined that she would do all the things that her neurosurgeon warned that she possibly might not do. Although at one point, Jayla stopped talking, became very distant, and totally unaffectionate. She started a habit of beating herself in the head and chest ferociously.

I still maintained my hope in God for her healing. This is the faith mindset that we, as Special Needs parents, caregivers, and everyone connected to these preciously created individuals, must embrace: we must hope against hope. No matter what it looks like, no matter how many times your heart breaks for them, and no matter how scary the diagnosis is, keep hope alive in your heart, your mind, and your soul. Speak The Word over your child or loved one. Decree the promises in His Word and declare positive affirmations daily. I am living proof that God will grant an abundance of His peace, gentleness, wisdom, and strength to provide the specialized care that your child or loved one requires.

A few weeks before her second birthday, a series of testing confirmed that she was on the Autism spectrum. This new diagnosis caused me to relive the same torment that I experienced when she had her first operation at seven weeks old. Was there something that I possibly could have done differently? Could I have taken another brand of prenatal vitamins? Could I have done anything at all to prevent her from being this way? I felt inadequate for giving my parents a granddaughter with Special Needs. I blamed myself for her having to undergo surgeries, therapy, and so many complications. I struggled with the heaviness of feeling like a disappointment to Jayla, my parents, and my family. I prayed so hard for understanding. My toughest obstacles taught me to truly **L.E.A.N.** on God by allowing Him to carry me through the hard days.

L: Let God take care of circumstances that are too much for you to handle. {1 Peter 5:7}
E: Expect God to answer when you pray, trust, and believe His Word. {Hebrews 11:1}
A: Accept the situations that you are not able to change. {1 Chronicles 16:11}
N: Never lose hope ~ instead, hold on to God's promises. {Romans 15:13}

We celebrated Jayla's sixth birthday, Easter, and Mother's Day in the hospital during a visit that lasted approximately two months. When she was released, I was exhausted in every area ~ spiritually, mentally, physically, and emotionally. Although we were home, my anxiety was still in constant overdrive due to being her mom, advocate, social worker, nurse, caregiver, guardian, and physical therapist. I was overexerted, overwhelmed, overpressured, and overcautious. As I lay there, I thought, "God, please help my mind rest." I made my requests known to Him by specifically stating what I needed in my fervent prayers. {Philippians 4:6} A few hours passed, I watched a couple of sitcoms, and it was almost time for Jayla's next dose of medication. As I tried to convince myself to get up, I whispered again, "Lord, help me! I wish there was a safe place that I could take her that would take care of her while I catch up on my rest and relax my mind."

Because I still felt incredibly drained. Yet and still, Jayla needed me, and I was certainly going to be there for her. Just as clear as the words you are reading right this moment, God began speaking to me, "You do it! Establish a community that embraces, encourages, and empowers Autism and Special Needs families. Build a support network for other mothers, family members, and caregivers who are feeling just like you are right now. Provide the quality service you are searching for. Offer them hope." At that precise moment, God granted me Green Light Grace as an Autism and Special Needs mom!

Have you ever been driving to work, church service, a doctor's appointment, or an important meeting, and you needed traffic to flow in perfect harmony to arrive on time? As you approach each intersection, you whisper a prayer to ask that the light synchronization works in your favor. You might even mentally cross your fingers, hoping that this small gesture will give your desperate appeal an express boost to Heaven so that God will answer speedily. I think we have all felt this way at least once, twice, or on numerous occasions in our lives.

In that very instant, it was as if God allowed all the lights on my journey to turn green at the same time, and *everything* unequivocally made sense! My tears, fears, and years of feeling helpless, guilty, and confused were all preparing me to help others. God suddenly shifted me from my broken mentality into my breakthrough mindset! He lifted my head. {Psalm 3:3} He supernaturally perfected my weaknesses with His strength. I clearly understood how His grace had been sufficient for me in every situation I faced as Jayla's mother.

"Each time, he said, "No. But I am with you; that is all you need. My power shows up best in weak people." Now I am glad to boast about how weak I am; I am glad to be a living demonstration of Christ's power, instead of showing off my own power and abilities. Since I know it is all for Christ's good, I am quite happy about "the thorn," and about insults and hardships, persecutions and difficulties; for when I am weak, then I am strong - the less I have, the more I depend on him."
{2 Corinthians 12:9-10 The Living Bible}

I felt His peace that surpasses all understanding when I began to realize just how many times He guarded my heart and kept my mind when I felt like falling apart. {Philippians 4:7} He gave me another victory! {1 Corinthians 15:57} That life-changing revelation from God was my Green Light Grace moment.

Now, I am ignited to embrace, equip, and empower mothers and entire families affected by Autism and Special Needs. It is my desire for every parent, grandparent, sibling, extended family member, caregiver, educator, and all other roles connected to this community to experience the same liberation God has given me. Never forget the amazing fact that God chose you to love and care for one of His uniquely designed individuals. Even with the myriad of twists and turns, ins and outs, ups and downs, and overs and unders, hope in God will lead you to your breakthrough. His grace is the key that unlocks the door that guides you to victoriously thriving in the role He has assigned to your life.

- Never give up; instead, give it all you have!
- Never breakdown for too long; instead, focus on figuring out how to breakthrough!
- Never be ashamed of your pain; instead, allow it to lead you on the path to your purpose.
- Although you may feel helpless at times, always remember you are never hopeless!

- God is always there, and I am here to walk alongside you on this journey to victorious living!

"Yes, you will suffer for a short time. But after that, God will make everything right. He will make you strong. He will support you and keep you from falling. He is the God who gives all grace. He chose you to share in his glory in Christ. That glory will continue forever."
{1 Peter 5:10 ERV}

About Shervondaline Sims Breedlove

    Shervondaline Sims Breedlove was born and raised in Monroe, Louisiana. She is the eldest of her parents' two children. Her Grammy began calling her a natural-born leader before turning a year old. She is an Autism Advocate, a Champion for Special Needs Parents and Families, 2X Bestselling Author,

Bestselling Visionary Anthologist, Entrepreneur, and Certified Spiritual Master Life Coach. She is passionate about establishing a thriving universal community of support for parents and families affected by Special Needs. Shervondaline has over 20 years of combined experience in Customer Care, Management, Finance, and Manufacturing with Fortune 500 Companies such as ConAgra, Chase, General Motors, and State Farm. Shervondaline earned her Bachelor's Degree in Christian Leadership and Community Organization from Integrity Seminary in Red Oak, Texas. Women Of Dignity Magazine has featured Shervondaline as Author of the Day, one of the 2022 Top 25 Rising Stars, and one of the 2022 Top Fifty Pioneers of Change.

Being a caring mother to her only daughter, Jayla, is one of her most fulfilling and rewarding roles. Their journey is a marvelous and miraculous testimony of love, resilience, expectation, courage, and restoration. Her motivation to provide guidance, help, and resources to individuals and families affected by Autism and Special Needs is fueled by their past experiences. Advocating for Autism for twenty-two years has equipped Shervondaline with a profound level of compassion, significant knowledge of the effects on the entire family, and a dynamic understanding of social functioning impacts.

God has mantled her to spread His Message of love, hope, strength, and healing to individuals and families affected by Special Needs. Shervondaline is a gifted Encourager. She is passionate about helping and comforting others on this journey which will motivate and inspire them to become more effective for Christ.

      Shervondaline knows the importance of always addressing situations with compassion and thoughtfulness. She believes that allowing people to see the authentic you will establish genuine connections that lead to relationships that will last a lifetime. Shervondaline loves sharing helpful tools, tips, and techniques vital for victorious living for the entire family. She has a servant's heart and is committed to being a blessing to others. Her greatest desire is to embrace, encourage, and elevate individuals and families within the Special Needs community through God's Word. Her number one priority is always leaving people better than she found them. Shervondaline truly understands firsthand that the people connected within this unique community are positively better together and wants to help them excel beyond their limitations.

      Shervondaline resides in Texas with her husband of 9 years, Arthur, and their daughter, Jayla. She enjoys traveling, decorating, reading, word games, and spending time with family and friends.

Connect with Shervondaline

Email: ssbreedlove220@gmail.com
Facebook: Shervondaline S. Breedlove
IG: authorssbreedlove

Glow In The Dark
By Jasbeen Singh

Have you ever felt like trying something new but then decided not to because you didn't have enough experience or information in that subject matter ... or maybe you're just too comfortable to make a move? You end up justifying the reasons you didn't take action to give you solace. You don't realize that when you didn't go for something you really wanted, you, in a sense, turned off the lights to that space in your heart, a space you had made when you first desired something, a wishful moment per se. Part of you will always wonder, "what if," which is why you gave it room in your heart in the first place. It's always going to be there, but the space remains dark. I want you to ask yourself - how many rooms remain dark in your heart?

We also tend to close the door to our dreams because of the daily hustle of life. Where does the hustle come from? Where does the "I don't have time for this" or "it's not for me" come from? As I've observed in life, we've let outside noise distort the truth, so much so that we trust people blindly and believe in everyone but ourselves. Why else do we put celebrities on pedestals and think they are "special" and that we can't ever achieve similar success? Just like the buzzing of bees, the distractions in our lives buzz around our minds and create clutter. We aren't able to think clearly. We are too consumed by the news, the internet, social media updates, and the barrage of expectations from everyone.

It's because everyone across social media channels are skewing "normal" with unrealistic fashion trends, financial advice, beauty, and social media standards, which are being advertised as real. So, we try to achieve what's unreal, and we never get close enough. In that rat race, we end up feeling like failures; we lose hope, often feel unworthy, stuck, and avoid taking further personal risks. We also don't advocate for ourselves as we should. We build resilience to an extent as well as tolerance for pain, but in the process, more and more rooms turn dark in our hearts. I invite you to look further. Where else have you turned off the switch because you were too scared to take the risk? Maybe you didn't have time or were intimidated by others. You didn't think you could do it or were afraid of the possible consequences…. if this happens, or if that…. Have you considered that all you had to be… was to be authentic. You don't have to fit in anywhere; you can just be you. Normal is where you are and how you are. Your interests, dreams, and goals are the news you need to follow!

I'm here to explain to you that life is a gift, and the act of getting up each day, determined to win, explore, shine, and share your gifts with the world, involves both risk and courage. Yes, there will be risks. Life is full of unknowns. Will that person like me, will they accept me, will I be safe, will it be worth it? You won't know until you challenge yourself, challenge the paradigms you've been living in, and challenge the status quo. Every day, the words echo in my mind when I think of Steve Harvey and his message about taking the jump. You have to jump - take that leap of faith. Trust God and go for it.

You have to be courageous. Life is LIFE when you LIVE it, not just exist through it. You need to experience the good, the bad, the exciting, and choose to be daring. The results from your experiences will teach you lessons to apply to future experiences. You will learn that you either don't like something or you LOVE something, but you won't know until you give it an effort. We did this as babies, toddlers, and kids, so why did we stop as adults?

Why sit on the sidelines and watch other people LIVE their lives? Want to learn how to swim? Put YOUR OWN feet in the water and experience your own thrills. Put the vest on and get in the water. What's the worst that can happen? Maybe you flop around in the water... but you may say people are watching... They don't know you! What are they going to do, write about you on their blog? When you go home that day, won't you feel exhilarated for having tried to do something that just hours before, you had only imagined? Every time you do something courageous like this, fear gets a little bit smaller each time, until eventually, fear disappears and what's left is a courageous and confident person embracing life.

      We need to be consciously aware of the thoughts we pay attention to. The thoughts that don't serve us - let them drift away like clouds. As dark clouds (thoughts) come in, acknowledge them as they come in but don't attach to them "hey, I see you... keep going... we've invited peace tonight!" You know you've been sucked in if you developed feelings because of those thoughts. This is hard work - real work - but life-saving work. Pay attention to your thoughts and only acknowledge and receive those that are positive, uplifting, encouraging, and God anointed. I promise you that nothing can stop you from achieving success, joy, love, peace, and happiness. All those other thoughts are just noise, keeping you from living your best life.

      While thoughts can be chosen, I certainly understand you may have had pain and suffering in life that you have endured, and I want to speak about that and give you a perspective to consider. Each time you went through pain, whether emotional pain, financial loss, or other tragedy, it probably stopped you in your tracks, I'm sure. You most likely felt a big rush of resistance pushing you from moving forward in your life. That resistance may have felt like a ton of bricks. You probably put up your hands and gave up during those times. You may have been surrounded by guilt, pain, loss, turmoil, and darkness. A force of gravity stopped you from going in the direction you thought your life was headed. And each time you went through another blow, a jab here and there, more bricks fell all around you. You probably did not realize that in those times, you didn't head in the direction you wanted to; God was lifting you higher and higher. Yes, there was a pile of mess underneath you, but you survived! And as those bricks fell, you climbed higher and higher. Your pain was not for nothing. God gave you a peak to look down from to clearly see all of the different paths that ARE available to you, the resources, the connections, the opportunities... and with this view, you can also acknowledge lessons learned, gain new insights, and/or embrace the cherished memories of your lost loved ones – taking all of this in to propel you into your purpose.

God created diversity in the world so that we could appreciate the beauty in others and appreciate the talents and gifts He gave us to share with the world. You weren't meant to follow the crowd. As Mr. Les Brown says to each person he meets, "There's greatness within you!" You were meant to do extraordinary things with your life, so let's stop letting life move us; let's move through life on our own terms. Let's follow our dreams, let's inspire our communities through our good work, let's uplift others, and bring joy to our friends and families. Be the guiding light for others. Live a life of purpose and meaning and positively impact the world. You don't have to feel overwhelmed anymore. Life's pressures are no more because you believe in yourself. You're going to be courageous and take risks; you're going to let negative thoughts drift away and take steps to achieve your dreams and goals. TURN ON ALL THE LIGHTS!!!!! WHOA!!!!!!!! FEEL THE EMOTIONS! Feel the chills in your arms! Let the light in your heart and spirit inside you inspire the world! Live your life!!!!!! Live it! Live it! Live it!

I want to share a quick story that really helped me to appreciate my life and gave me even more inspiration to achieve my goals, and it has to do with glowing in the dark. I was blessed to go to India with my family in early 2022.

During the pilgrimage, I took part in while there, I brought about a huge commotion. A large crowd ascended on me when I busted out tubes of glow sticks to pass out to children. Yes, I created a commotion, lol! I purchased two glow sticks tubes through Amazon; each tube had 100 glow sticks. I packed them for the trip with a heart eager to bring smiles to India - and I brought more than just smiles. Glow sticks aren't as common there as you would find here. In the U.S., about every theme park, county fair, or even dollar store has glow sticks. Where I had taken them to in India, we had been in rural areas, and it was the first time anyone ever saw or held one.

Many people thought these were magical bracelets and would push their hands through the crowd eager to get one, both young and old alike. At first, it was going great, and then as people advertised the source of the contraption, a few kids turned into scores of people hovering around me for an opportunity to get one. My husband just watched from a distance, chuckling and not offering to help since it was my own doing. It was pretty simple, crack and bend, add the connector and hand it out. It was getting the connector in that was difficult because those little pieces were in a separate little baggie. When the tube emptied, the disappointed few would light up when others shared theirs with them. I gave myself a break the second night and took out the last tube on the third night of the pilgrimage. I had become savvy and cracked and connected them before passing them out! It was so cool that even though the glow dissipated the next day, people wore them proudly for days.

    I really enjoyed this experience because as we were there to pray and visit temples, the community of people we were surrounded with was proudly displaying their bracelets. I had been passing them out at nighttime, where we would convene outside under the open sky on the grounds of the temples we visited. When religious hymns were playing, and everyone would sit around and clap in unison, all you could see in the dark were colorful halos glowing and dancing in the dark all around. It was simply magical. The bracelets indeed had become magical in a sense. I give all glory to God. While it was a simple act of kindness, God added such beauty to the celebrations. The bracelets were more than something cool and new; to me, they represented God's Light, a discovery as this was new and exciting for so many people, but also a source of inspiration and wonderment. As we gathered to pray and sing praises to God, the glowing bracelets represented hope and God's shower of love and light on His devotees. Everyone felt a higher level of spiritual enlightenment, and the glow sticks brought all our hearts together.

In India, I also witnessed the resilience of the people I met. The traffic there was crazy. Anything with one or multiple wheels would compete to move ahead of the other, and they ALL seemed to have invisible bumpers. They would maneuver like "Fast and Furious" at times or swarm in unison, but they always kept inches away from one another. As energetic, loud, and busy traffic was, equally peaceful were the serene farmlands where all you heard were birds chirping, cows occasionally mooing, wheat fields whistling through the breeze, and light splashes of water in the tube wells. Whether in the loud city streets or quiet farmlands, I witnessed the strength of the people and how content they were with their work and circumstances, despite appearing incredibly difficult and different to westerners like me.

All day long, local shops would splash buckets of water on the road in front of their stores to prevent dust on their products or produce (we take garden hoses for granted here!). When we went to clothing stores, looking for Punjabi suits or other materials to have sewn, the shop owners would create heaping piles of materials they opened up to show us. It would build up anxiety in me just looking at the work ahead of them after we would leave, and despite insisting they not open any additional designs, they would more than happily do so. Farmers would spend hours in the hot sun and with pride as every task would lead them to a hopeful harvest. Restaurants would have employees standing around the food table to be available at a customer's call, in case more Rotis, beverages, or anything else was needed. The bathrooms in some of these establishments were so pristine, and they took pride in creating a memorable experience. They would wait on patrons just outside in case any additional toiletries may be needed. It seemed that being patient and doing tedious & repetitive tasks weren't seen as a chore, instead were woven into the fabric of their routine and, ultimately, the success of a sale.

When I came back home, I realized how different our lifestyles are here vs. the people I met in India. Here, people, in general, can become so unhappy in life, despite having comfortable lives and possessions that others in the world would consider luxuries. We are so eager for instant gratification that there is often very little patience for tedious or repetitive tasks. We do many things and keep busy, but none of the million things are towards a single purpose. I observed people doing many things in India but towards a single purpose. Sure, with some equipment, they can be a little more efficient (garden hose), but no one seemed to be stressed out, and they were living content lives within their means. I took away the importance of being patient, being of service, and working towards a goal.

As I pondered on that notion - instant gratification - I was reminded of the glow sticks and the instant glow once activated. Just like glow sticks, I believe that we must make a committed decision (snap glow stick) to achieve our personal desires and goals. A committed decision does not have back-pocket exit channels; you must commit to your decision. Once you've made a commitment to yourself, take in the glow, and fill your heart with the light. Remain committed to your goal each day. Envision your end goal being complete, and let that feeling of pride, excitement, and accomplishment run through your veins. See the instant glow, not as instant gratification, because it may take days or months for you to achieve it, but let that glow serve to fuel your spirit with hope and courage.

You see, once you glow, others will be inspired to glow. And just like my experience at the mountain top during the pilgrimage, the combined glow from everyone lifted all of us up even higher than we would have done so alone. You have one life, one chance to play the role God gave you to be you. Are you going to just observe others being them, or will you take a chance at seeing what you can do? Light up all your rooms in your heart! Be determined to live your best life! Let's snap it up and light it up! Dare to glow in the dark and move towards your dreams!

About Jasbeen Singh

Jasbeen Singh is a proud mother of two children and a devoted wife residing in Elk Grove, California.

She is an expert in coaching individuals and inspiring them to be the best version of themselves. Her career includes 25 years of customer service experience, with the last two decades as a public servant and call center manager in State Government.

She shares her personal breakthrough story in the Women of Power Voice anthology and continues to delve into inspirational writing. She shares further insight on how to live our best lives in her chapter in the Ignited to Serve Anthology.

It's her mission in life to be of service to people of all ages, and she does that by sharing her stories as an aspiring author. You can find more information about her upcoming projects, including her personal memoir and children's books, by visiting www.jasbeeninspires.com.

You can also reach her through her Facebook page at https://www.facebook.com/JasbeenInspires

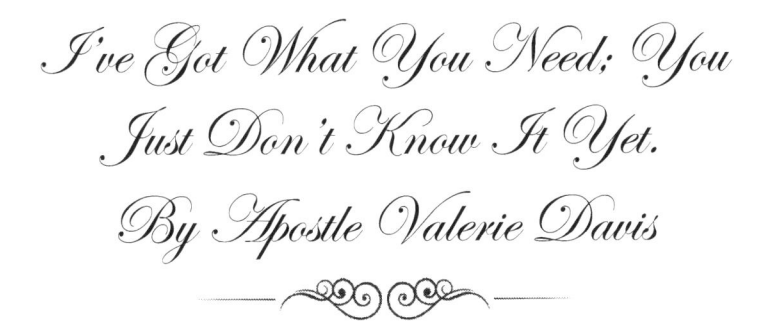

I've Got What You Need; You Just Don't Know It Yet.
By Apostle Valerie Davis

I've found it interesting how you start with a plan and how God intercepts with His plan, one that you've not even conceived. Scripture says, *man makes their plans, but God orchestrates the events of your life.* Proverbs 16:9.

I've always seemed to understand the power of service as it was instilled in me by my parents from the time that I could understand speech and literature. You see, I was a minister's baby. My parents were married in the church office, and my father was the chairman of the deacon's board for many years. As early as I can remember, I was taught about service, whether giving in tithes, serving in capacities in the local church or school, or local organizations, I may have been involved in. Service and assistance to others were made a priority and focal point in my home.

Often, I resented my parents for the push in this regard as I noticed that service of any kind required time, energy, and effort, which sometimes I was not always willing to commit to in my youth. I think of early mornings getting to Sunday school to assist in class or choir and usher duties. I felt that my parents were just too immersed in the church and all the activities. I remember my mom teaching my brother and I about service to our residential neighbors as well. There were a couple of neighbors who had lots of children, and my mother mentioned that they might need additional support.

My family consisted of my mother, father, older brother, and myself. My father was a relatively successful businessman in Chicago, and monetary resources were not a problem in our home. This, my parents, instilled through their actions that assistance would be required when we saw a need and could help. Scripture says, *to whom much is given, much is required,* St. Luke 12:48.

I found myself braiding neighborhood children's hair on my porch, sharing toys, piggy bank money, and other resources. This, in turn, instilled so much in me, such as a sense of community and connectivity to others, also imparted within me a knowledge and understanding that we are all interconnected. What we make happen for others, we, in turn, serve ourselves. It opened me up to be less selfish and self-serving. I became more empathetic and compassionate of others and their plights and conditions. Marian Wright Edelman, one of the great educators of our time, stated, "Service is the rent we pay for being." It is the very purpose of life and not something you do in your spare time."

The great orator and Civil Rights Leader Martin Luther King said it best, "Not everyone can be famous, but everyone can be great because greatness is determined by service."

All these great attributes and good character qualities were instilled in me; however, I began to veer off onto a different path as I matured and was not as involved with spiritual things. My focus became more self-serving and selfish as I pressed for more independence. I stopped attending church and filled my time with work and clubbing. Don't get me wrong, I still served and helped others but just not as much. I always had a penchant and knack for acquiring good employment opportunities, which I now know as Favor. I found myself helping others get good employment opportunities and placements. I've always wanted to see others advance as I grew.

However, my life decisions and choices began to manifest options I wasn't ready for. I realized that though I was fortunate to have both of my parents for many years, who made positive impartation, I was still broken and had experienced brokenness which opened me up to areas of deficiencies that would ultimately alter my life adversely for a season. We've often heard the scripture which states, "the wages of sin is death." I had heard this so often in church as a young person, but it was now becoming more apparent as life happened, and my views became more skewed and compromised.

I have found that painful life experiences tend to cloud good judgment and often alter vision and right perception. I was carrying baggage that was preventing me from arising to soar in my life. I did not realize that until certain things are fully realized and recognized as toxic and emitted from your life naturally and spiritually, you can find yourself stuck in a rut for years. Though you may be a great person with great attributes, skills, and abilities to help yourself and others, it is often hindered and made to be inoperable due to personal, internal, and limiting mindsets that must be demolished.

It seemed that serving came so easy in my youth. It seemed less laborious and was an added joy; however, as a young woman, I saw it as more tedious and oftentimes complicated, as service to others many times required something given of yourself in time, money or talent, and skills of which I felt I had limited amounts of to share and give, or so I thought. The limiting and deficit mindset would have you believe you have a limited supply of and just enough for yourself and the immediate persons you choose to supply.

These unproductive mindsets were evident as a result of me carrying weights from past hurts, disappointments, frustrations, and even unforgiveness that limited my abilities to fully serve myself and others adequately. I became limited in my scope and vision to see serving others as a source of fulfillment and contentment. It was not until God fully restored me in my soul that the meaning of service and real care for others became significant to me. For service to be impactful, it must be done with a willingness of heart and mind. This, of course, can only become possible when we truly allow our hearts to become synchronized to the will of God. Serving must become a mission of purposefulness.

I have come to realize in my time in the pastorate, that life and all the things we experience and are able to weather through have all been for the purpose of serving others. It is for the purpose of being a blessing to others around me. Apostle Paul stated in St. Luke 22:31-34, *when thou art strengthen or made whole, one art to strengthen thy brethren.* God has made us to live, move and have our being in Him, and He requires us to think in terms of serving with a purpose.

The Lord is now gathering like-minded women and men in this hour like Prophet Nehemiah stated in Nehemiah 4:6, "People joined together," the people had a mind to work. In this day and time, it will take purpose pushers, destiny helpers, and vision casters to come alongside certain works and lend their talent, voices, time, and resources to see things come into full manifestation in each of them our lives. God never designed us to do it alone. No longer will we treasured vessels be content to sit alongside, letting others go ahead of us to do, but God is thrusting us forth to initiate, implement and facilitate programs, services, and events that will benefit mankind.

God is looking for willing servants who are desirous to be change agents on the earth, filled with hearts and minds ready to serve without hesitation or reservation. When you are filled with the passion for purpose, it causes an excitement and expectation in the heart that cannot be dampened, and it lights a spark of hopefulness for favorable outcomes. This synergy, when encountered by others, becomes irresistible and undeniable. It is like a flame of fire. It connects and catches on wherever one goes. I'd like to think of it as the frequency you carry in life. I believe that what we carry can be transferable. So, what we empower our lives with must be examined and guarded. This is the reservoir we build within us, preparing us to be able to be poured out and be again replenished for future service.

About Valarie Davis

Apostle/Prophetess Valerie Davis serves as Senior Pastor alongside her husband, Apostle Steven Davis, of Greater Works Evangelism Church in Chicago, Ill. She served faithfully several years under the leadership of Apostle John Eckhardt of Crusaders Ministries in capacities as Team leader of Presbytery and prophetic teams, teacher, and elder.

Because of Apostle Davis genuine concern for the spiritual development and equipping of women and young people for ministry and life, she implemented Women Called to Win (WCTW). Her emphasis through WCTW is to train, equip, and provide personal development counsel/therapy designed to help others materialize the manifestation of goals and vision. She is also dedicated to providing through the teaching of God's word wisdom, knowledge, exhortation, and counsel to all those that come into her midst.

Apostle Davis ministers under a strong prophetic, healing, deliverance, and psalmist anointing that has been effectual in catapulting the lives of those who receive into greater dimensions of fruitfulness and effectiveness. Her simplistic messages, sparked by her energy, wisdom, and love for God's word and His people, have made her a sought-after and well-received speaker and minister. This is also evident in her travels as she is convinced of the call to the nations; she has traveled extensively in the United States, South Africa, Ethiopia, and the Caribbean.

Apostle Davis has an Associates of Arts Degree in Liberal Arts, Bachelors of Arts Degree in Organizational Management & Leadership, and Master of Arts Degree in Forensic Psychology. Prophetess Davis is employed as a Clinical Care Manager at a Healthcare Company in Chicago.

It's Always Darkest Before The Dawn
By Susan Hall

On November 2, 1996, I found myself once again at the altar, about to embark on my third marriage. I, like multiple other young women everywhere, in love with the idea of what I had always dreamed marriage would be. We often think of a beautiful little family with a white picket fence and dreamy, but here I was, still a broken and co-dependent woman who simply didn't want to be alone. Had I known at that moment what I know now, even leaning over to my soon-to-be husband and whispering in his ear, "what in the world are we doing right now?" I probably wouldn't have done it! My husband had never been married before; I already had four sons, so we immediately had a blended family.

Our first ten years were far from what I had always envisioned for my life.

I truly believed that because my husband was a Bible college graduate that somehow I would never face some of the things I ended up facing.

The first time I discovered he was having an affair, I was completely shocked and devastated. I took it completely personally, believing I was the problem.

I centered my life around trying to control and fix everything co-dependency had been my partner in life, and I constantly walked on eggshells. Basing my happiness on if he was happy, I was happy; if he was upset, then I would be upset. I had lost my true identity, and I knew I had to fight for myself and fight for my marriage.

We had a history together; I knew he was a good-willed man who was broken and needed to be free.

Things began to take a turn one day as I realized that I could only work on myself.

I had such a spirit of rejection, and I knew I had to break out of it somehow.

I stood for my marriage even when everyone told me I was crazy and it would never change. I spoke only what I wanted to see, "Faith is calling those things that be not as though they already are." -Romans 4:17

I declared that my marriage was restored, even when it looked beyond hopeless.

I allowed God to heal me fully and began to see myself as He saw me – beautifully and wonderfully created.

Remember, "It's always darkest before the dawn." You are on the very threshold of a breakthrough, precious one. Do not give up now; everything is subject to change!

Why do you think Satan has attacked your life so much? Because you are valuable. You are more valuable than gold. You are a beautiful story to share, and it must be written. Your assignment is valuable; your dreams are valuable!

On November 2, 2021, we celebrated our 25th wedding anniversary. To say we have had restoration is truly an understatement.

What do you do when you don't know what to do? When you're broken? When you feel like you're not enough?

1-Don't give up 2-You are more than enough! You are precious and beautiful, and you are more than desiring to live. You are totally accepted by God. You have purpose.

What does my life look like today? Is it perfect? - far from it, but I'm so grateful I did not throw in the towel many years ago.

Three and a half years ago, I, along with my husband, took on the responsibility of raising one of our grandbabies. At the time, he was nine weeks old. It hasn't been easy but I am doing what God has called me to do in this season; he is worth it.

My husband, of course, is a powerhouse for men that struggle with addictions. He and I teach and do talks on restoration for your marriage, relationships, financial freedom, counseling with couples, and speaking engagements.

If I could tell one thing to women who are going through a similar situation, I would say you must get off of the "roller coaster ride" and make the decision to take back your life. Never allow your identity to be tainted by someone else's issues. You can do it, and you have what it takes to put that faith into action! I believe in you!!!

About Susan Hall

Sometimes life throws us curve balls that we think we can never overcome, Believing that it will and cannot ever change. Susan was so Co-dependent, and she lived her life basing her happiness on what the day would bring, whether good or bad. Years ago, Susan settled for whatever she could get, especially in her marriage, and she allowed the opinions of others to dictate who she was. Susan had lost the real her and began to believe that she had to earn love and acceptance instead of realizing that she was already loved and fully accepted by God. Susan found herself in need of total restoration and healing. Today, Susan is an entirely different person, She knows who she is, and more importantly, she knows whose she is. Week after week, she encourages precious women to find out their true identity and see themselves as beautiful and precious to God. Restoration is her passion, and her husband of 25 years now.

Today, Susan stands here not perfect but as a Trophy of God's never-ending love and Grace. Never believe that you are ever too far to reach. You are just one step away. ♥ You are love!

Contact Susan

Email: susanhjayne@icloud.com

Phone: 918-402-2897

YouTube Channel "James and Susan Hall Ministries"

The Power of You!
By Valila Wilson

Reflections

I remember a little girl whose innocence was stolen from her. From the age of five to eight, she had to endure sexual molestation and abuse induced by a few of her family members. She kept it quiet partly out of fear and partly out of naivety. This was the same little broken-hearted seven-year-old daddy's girl who no longer felt unique or valued because she had lost something precious and significant. It had profoundly affected her. She once had a tight-knit relationship and bond with her father. However, this once close, loving, nurturing, and beautiful father-daughter relationship became toxic in the blink of an eye. Her hero had now become detached, distant, critical, judgmental, and unpleased with her. Confused and stunned, she was clueless about what she had done to cause the person who was the center of her world to reject and emotionally abandon her. His once loving words had transformed into sharp daggers that left violent gnashes and deep penetrating rips in her soul. She was devastated and lost. She was no longer Daddy's

"Sweet Pea." This abused and discarded little daddy's girl was me.

As I embark upon celebrating my fabulous 49th birthday, I cannot help but seriously reflect on the woman I have become. It has caused me to realize the magnitude of what I have had to overcome to be free and currently walk in my God-given purpose and calling as a Woman of Power. I have had some major battles. I mean an all-out knock-down, drag-out war in which I have had to fight for my life on several occasions. I have discovered how many of my issues throughout my life were rooted in the early childhood traumas I shared with you. I had to get free and overcome my past and the rotten fruit it produced.

Despite the many loving, healthy, encouraging, and uplifting relationships I had with my family outside those who were abusers, I still had struggles well into my adulthood. As a result of the trauma I had endured, I developed seven distinct driving forces: an inferiority complex, approval addiction, low self-esteem, low self-worth, a lack of self-love, and later the imposter syndrome. This caused me to put on a façade and live disingenuously so that I would feel better about myself. I wore a mask and did what I thought would bring acceptance and approval. I was not the authentic Valila. This caused me to struggle with success in my relationships, career, responsibilities, and personal well-being. I was stifled and struggled with adding significant value to the communities I served. The Power of Me was fleeting and a mere shadow. Even though I knew I was created for greatness, I was not powerful. I hungered to be all that God had designed me to be. I had become passionate about being The Woman of Power God had purposed me to be. So what brought about the change in my status as a "Woman of Power?" I discovered the Power of Me, and you can discover the Power of You.

Understanding and Activating The Power of You

"The Power of You is in the *Being*."

Being Authentically You

If we are going to be a woman of power, we must be AUTHENTIC. If we are going to be authentic, we must start with the gift of The Truth – God's Truth. If this gift is handled appropriately, it will bring about the freedom to be our authentic selves and be victorious at it. The Truth will produce liberty and transformation. The Truth will align us with our authentic selves, activating our God-given power.

According to God's Word, Psalms 139:13, 14, we are fearfully and wonderfully made. God's works are Marvelous. I had heard this scripture repeatedly, but the light came on one day. Listen, God did not just slap some cells together, and there was something called you. No, No, No! God took His time and thoughtfully DESIGNED you. Your personality, smile, skin, lips, legs, natural aroma, temperament, etc., are carefully created to be uniquely you. You are a Designer Brand passionately created by the Most High God.

So, when you are trying to be a cheap copy/knock-off of someone else, you are not being the authentic designer brand of *you*. We are not operating in our God-given Power when we are trying to be like someone else. When we walk in our true selves, we begin to flow in our God-given abilities to dominate naturally (influence and lead), subdue (conquer), multiply (increase, abundance, excel), replenish (to fill or fulfill, finish), and be fruitful (bring forth, cause to grow or increase, produce). Although God gave us all this ability, how we flow in it is unique to each individual. When we learn to be our authentic selves, we unlock a power that will serve others and add value to everything we do. We then go from being blessed to BEING The BLESSING. This is the Power of You being Activated.

Being a Vessel of God

I have a god-sister that always says, "I am just a vessel." She always reminds us in the sisterhood that we are just vessels. One particular morning we were talking, and I requested prayer. I shared the assignment that I had accepted from God. I was saying that I did not feel worthy of the assignment in so many words. Yep, that old inferiority complex was in effect. She respectfully cut me off and proceeded, "Move yourself out the way. You are just a vessel."

All I could say was, "Amen," because my spirit had been pricked at that moment. For several Days, God dealt with me about what it meant to be a vessel of His. It is like my god-sister said. First, you must move *you* out of the way. In other words, we cannot allow all our flaws, inadequacies, character defects, and struggles to get in the way of us doing the good work He has chosen us to do. When God chose you, He knew what / who He was getting.

Also, when we are speaking of moving ourselves out of the way, we need not allow all our "I don't want to's," personal hang-ups, and pet peeves to stop us from doing the assignment God has chosen us for. Once we have moved out of the way and given God our "yes," we are to yield to Him and follow His leading to accomplish the good work we were chosen to do.

When we are our true selves, God can more effectively use us to be a vessel of blessing. We become a powerful instrument of God for His kingdom. This Glorifies God, and now we are fulfilling our primary purpose according to Isaiah 43: 7- to glorify God.
Being the Authentic You and Being a Vessel of God produces "The Power of You" to do great works for the Kingdom of God.

Beware of The Opposition

The Power of You is fulfilled when the authentic you is in the Master's Hands, being used for the good works you were created for. It is about yielding and becoming a vessel of God for His purpose. But I must warn you that there is strong opposition set forth by the enemy to neutralize and deactivate The Power of You. I believe there are seven primary opponents/oppositions that I need to make you aware of and how to overcome them. This is not to say that there aren't more opponents. However, these are the primary 7 I continuously witness individuals facing and need to walk in victory over. There is a Power Strategy we can use to overcome the enemy as he tries to use these seven opponents to steal, kill, and destroy.

Oppositions
1. _Victim Mentality_ is an acquired personality trait in which a person tends to recognize or consider themselves a victim of the negative actions of others. People with a victim mentality believe that all their failings and misfortunes can be blamed on someone or something else. They believe they have no control over things that happen to them.
2. _Inferiority Complex_ is an intense personal feeling of inadequacy, often resulting in the belief (deriving from actual or imagined) that one is in some way deficient or inferior to others. At its core, it is a feeling used to convey a strong sense of being less than or not enough.
3. _Imposter Syndrome_ is the persistent inability to believe that one's success is deserved or has been legitimately achieved as a result of one's own efforts or skills. The individual tends to have a perpetual belief that they are not as competent as others perceive them to be.

They often experience feelings of being a phony, and they will be found out to be a fraud at any moment.
4. *Flea Syndrome* is when someone, through conditioning, tends to live under limiting beliefs even when those conditions are no longer a reality. Sometimes the limiting beliefs, unknowingly, are passed down.
5. *Ignorance* is a lack of knowledge or information.
6. *Approval Addiction* is a term used to describe a condition in which someone puts pleasing others above their own needs, "people-pleasing."
7. *Fear of Rejection* is the being afraid of not being liked, accepted, abandoned, not fitting in, or being alone. There is a fear of being seen in a critical way.

The Power Strategy of Truth

This Power Strategy is anchored in The Truth of God's Word. Jesus used the Word of God to overcome the enemy. He submitted unto God, resisted the devil, and caused the devil to flee. This was Jesus' power strategy, and it worked every time. The strategy is simple.

- **Learn The Truth of God's Word**. What God says is true and is the only thing that really matters. Yes, the facts are the facts, but what does God say about the facts of the matter?

- **Believe The Truth of God's Word**. God's truth has power over the facts. Take notice of the facts but bring them under the power of God's truth. Trust God and His word to be true no matter what it seems, feels, or looks like.
- **Confess The Truth in Word and Deed**. Make sure your words are saying what God says is true. Therefore, you must learn The Truth. You must speak life (What God says) and not death (negativity). Do not receive or agree with anything outside of what God's word has said. Do not allow others to speak over you anything outside of The Truth. Take note that your confessions are not only spoken but are also demonstrated in your actions. By the grace of God and the empowerment of the Holy Spirit, align your behavior with your confessions with The Truth.

Overcoming the Opponents

If you struggle with any of these opponents/oppositions, I want you to shout and dance. That's right, shout and dance because you can get free and have the victory IN JESUS NAME! **You can overcome them by applying The Power Strategy of Truth.** Now understand that you will have to put in the work if you want to get free and be the woman of power you were designed to be. First, research the opponent and then learn what God's words say about the opponent. Next, you must choose that no matter what, you will believe and trust

God's word about you concerning the opposition you are facing. This next step is crucial. You must confess The Truth *in word and deed*. Align your words and actions with what God says and do not receive or accept anything else. The opposition is real, but You Can Overcome it! You are Victorious! Remember...

Being Authentically You + Being a Vessel of God =

The Power of You.

In Jesus' Name

Become "A WOMAN OF POWER, IGNITED TO SERVE"

Amen

About Valila Wilson

Valila Wilson is a powerhouse woman of skill, experience, gifts, and passion that all converge into one life mission: transformation. Valila is a Success Empowerment Agent with a simple yet astounding formula – Success = Purpose Accomplished.

Her goal is to add value to everything she encounters through her gifts and callings as a speaker, coach, author, trainer, intercessor, community leader, evangelist, teacher, marketplace minister, and kingdom entrepreneur. Valila is a champion for those who are hurting, broken, and mistreated.

Valila's roots in leadership, business, and empowerment began deep in her ancestry with a grandparent who trailblazed entrepreneurship in their community for African Americans. She has taken that foundation and built an empire of her own that includes her learning from some of the best in community and business leadership. Valila has a BA in Psychology; is a Maxwell Leadership Certified speaker, coach, and trainer. She is also certified in business management with over three decades of experience. She is an ordained Evangelist and Minister and the founder of Essentially Beautiful Women's Ministry, Creations By Design, and Success Empowerment. She's dedicated her life and livelihood to helping others experience sustainable success through a strategic focus on personal, professional, and leadership development. Valila helps others "unlock the eagle within" and empowers them to soar in Success = Purpose Accomplished by discovering and believing in themselves.

Valila is a visionary – a woman dedicated to her own healing journey, wholeness, self-discovery, and learning to cultivate and express her own beauty and strength. She is an advocate for those who need to be reminded of who they are and whose they are. Valila is a lover of art in all its forms – creative, musical, and performance. She is an intercessor and evangelist in every arena of life. From her community outreach efforts to her professional career endeavors, she can always be found doing God's work through her callings. Valila is a leader with over 35 years of leadership experience in ministry, business, and entrepreneurship. Valila is an authenticity champion – helping people peel back the layers of lies and misconceptions that life may have given them to reveal their true, authentic selves and set them on a trajectory toward success.

Valila is a dedicated and loving mother of two sons. She loves to read, write, and take advantage of every opportunity she finds to pour into the lives of others. She loves the wintertime, laughter, and having a genuinely good time. As hard as she works, she also loves to rest and relax with a good tv show or a mystery novel. More than anything, Valila is committed to connecting to others deeply and creating disciples, while encouraging and training those she touches to do the same.

Set On Fire
By Latisha Shearer

When a woman gives birth to something or someone, a previous event must first occur for her to become impregnated. Many celebrate the baby's birth but tend to forget the overactive bladder, the morning sickness, the stretch marks, countless doctor appointments, and being always sleepy, hungry, and feeling hot. We forget something first took place before the birthing. Likewise, we often see women ignited to serve, and we forget that something first had to occur to set them on fire. Somewhere in life, the heat got too hot, and the flame needed fuel to ignite.

How are fires started? I am glad you asked. A fire triangle, also known as a combustion triangle, consists of three components required to ignite and sustain a fire. The three components required are heat, fuel, and oxygen; the fire will be extinguished without either one of these components. So, what were the heat, fuel, and oxygen that ignited the fire in me to serve?

Heat

Heat develops when the amount of energy is transferred from a system to the surrounding area due to a temperature difference. My life took a temperature change through several circumstances and mentalities. There are times when I mute myself to avoid sounding like a "Me Too Campaign" and "I can one-up you." However, I can empathize with those that have been molested because five different individuals molested me. I can relate to those that have been raped because I have been gang-raped twice within the same month of graduating from high school. After witnessing someone being killed, I can understand those with post-traumatic stress disorder because I faced it at fifteen. I know what it is like to have 'daddy issues' because my dad denied me as his child. I still feel the rejection of my siblings for being an outside child. I relate to the promiscuous woman or teen because I was a stripper, prostitute, and committed infidelity numerous times. Though addiction comes in many forms, I understand the stronghold of drugs, pills, and alcohol to ease the pain that kept me a prisoner of war in my mind. Money problems: bankruptcy, foreclosure, payday loans, and living check to check, yes, me too. I have experienced issues in my marriage that would shake any foundation and would have led to a divorce. Health issues, combat veteran, and military spouse yeah, let's not begin to go there!!

    So yes, I jam all these things and more in a bottle, closing the cap but the stench of my contents showed in my speech, mentalities, and relationships. I had the type of heat that was adjusting the temperature in my life. In the process of dealing and coping, I misdiagnosed my mentality of 'ignore and override' as being resilient. I was loud and wrong, declaring that I was resilient when in all actuality, I was vulnerable and caught behind enemy lines of the issues in my mind. I usually could adapt as I chose not to deal with a particular situation or suppress my feelings. However, the fuel came adding another source to the fire triangle.

Fuel

Women tend to hold everything together, and it seems as though one more can send everything crashing down. Being essentially homeless was the additional incident that prompted the entire frame to collapse. After quickly selling our house and trying to relocate to another state, buying a home became very challenging. The process of purchasing a house can be time-consuming. We went through the process twice; unfortunately, the appraisal returned less than the asking price a week before closing. Both times the sellers refuse to go down on the asking price to the appraised amount. Therefore, my family was in and out of hotels and Airbnb for three months.

The stress of this situation causes me to go into a mental breakdown. Being new to the area, by the time I got into the VA, I was out of some of my medications for depression, anxiety, and low on others. At this point, I felt like I was losing my mind. After several failed attempts by the Social Worker and Psychiatrist to get me to self-admit myself to the VA for a short stay for mental health, I found strength in telling them about the omnipotence of God and quickly departed the clinic.

I became outraged with battling depression. I was fed up with my past having a stronghold over me. I became weary of crying over spilled milk. I was annoyed with myself for allowing others' actions and words to have more value than it was worth in my life. I had enough of wanting and needing to feel accepted by friends, family, and associates only to be rejected. Something had to change; my mindset had to shift. My mental breakdown became the fuel to my fire.

Oxygen

Without oxygen, the carbon combustion, the fire will be extinguished. Instead of relying on prescriptions and other substances to sustain me, I began to take in the breath of God. God became the oxygen that I needed and desired. In my previous mental state, who God created me to be would have never ignited without the breath of God blown into me. I was overheating and felt suffocated by life circumstances before, but as Job 33:4 states, "For the Spirit of God has made me, and the breath of the Almighty gives me life." I knew the Word, but I had to release all the garbage that I was holding on to and allow the Word to get deeper into me. I had to begin to speak the Word of God and positive affirmations over myself three times a day to shift my mindset.

As my mind shifted and I came out of the grave I was buried in, I was ignited to go back with a shovel and dig other women out. I became a woman ignited to serve the broken in spirit. Remind them *The Lord is close to the brokenhearted; he rescues those whose spirits are crushed.* I became a woman ignited to strengthen women on the battlefield in their minds who feel as though they are trapped behind enemy lines. I can now say that it was good that I was afflicted because now that I have grown through what I had to go through, I am a woman ignited to serve. Apostle Peter in 1 Peter 5:10 states, *So after you have suffered a little while, He will restore, support, and strengthen you, and He will place you on a firm foundation.* The Apostle give these words from experience because he was told to go back and strengthen the brethren after being sifted as wheat. (Luke 22:31-34). I am ignited to serve other women because I have been sifted as wheat.

If you are currently feeling the heat and fuel of life circumstances, allow God's Word to be the oxygen that sets you ablaze, igniting you to serve. Inhale the Word of God into your spirit by taking it in daily before you put anything else into your mind, body, soul, and spirit. Before you conversate with anyone else, converse with God. Do a self-evaluation on how you are speaking to yourself. If you are speaking negatively, then change how you talk to yourself and about yourself to others. Often, we are disrespectful in the way we communicate with ourselves but demand respect from everyone else that we encounter.

Philippians 4:8 states, *"And now, dear brothers and sisters, one final thing. Fix your thoughts on what is true, and honorable, and right, and pure, and lovely, and admirable. Think about things that are excellent and worthy of praise."* Watch what you allow into your spirit. It is okay to feel, but do not allow what you feel to consume you. Process your emotions and then release them. Remember, it is not when a ship enters inside of water that it sinks, but when the water enters the ship that results in sinking. Remember, you are God's vessels, do not allow attitudes, negativity, emotions, and circumstances to cause you to sink.

Prophesy the Word of God over your life. Mediate on Ezekiel 37: 9-10. *Then he said to me, Speak a prophetic message to the winds, son of man. Speak a prophetic message and say, 'This is what the Sovereign Lord says Come, O breath, from the four winds! Breathe into these dead bodies so they may live again. So, I spoke the message as He commanded me, and breath came into their bodies. They all came to life and stood up on their feet—a great army."*

It is time for us to come out of the graveyard with dry bones. Each of us is vital to the army of the Lord, and we need to speak life into each other, commanding these dry bones to live. I speak boldly and prophetically to the four winds; that breath will come into each one of you that you may live again. Remember as you are strengthened, as you are restored, as you are ignited, go and serve other women.

About Latisha Shearer

Prophetess Latisha Shearer is uniquely anointed to create, mentor, and equip leaders and spiritual warriors in the body of Christ. She is a dynamic and highly skilled leader who will thrive in challenging mindset shifts to promote inner healing and deliverance. Helping those trapped behind the enemy lines in their minds escape and be set free.

Having endured trauma on a multifaceted level, Prophetess Shearer speaks at women's conferences with a passion for guiding and empowering attendees to confront and process their emotions and admit to themselves that inner healing needs to take place. She then challenges them to confront the flesh, guides them into the decision to forgive themselves and others, and engage in deeper intimacy with God the Father, Son, and Spirit.

As the visionary of Fervently Creations Christian Talk Show which streams on tv and radio, Prophetess Shearer transparently addresses other traumas like anxiety, substance abuse, sexual trauma, depression, and more in her continuing efforts to focus on inner healing and deliverance. Prophetess Shearer believes in promoting others and uses her platforms as an avenue for marketplace ministry.

As an inspiring author and teacher dedicated to seeing people grow through adversity, Prophetess Shearer has never stopped learning. She first obtained a B.S. in Religion Evangelism with a minor in Christian counseling. An M.A. in Biblical Exposition, and is currently pursuing a Doctor of Ministry with a concentration in Biblical Studies, all at Liberty University in Lynchburg, Va.

She has been ignited to serve by developing Bible studies for both children and adults, counseling, conference speaker, praise dance ministry leader for both young and adults, etc.

As the visionary of a Y.A.M. (Young Adult Ministry), Prophetess Shearer gave young adults, ages 18 to 35, a safe place to grow and be educated with the teaching of the Word on different life challenges. With enthusiasm about the church's future leaders, she served youth as a Bible Study and Vacation Bible School teacher. Also, Prophetess Shearer has served as Armor-Bearer, facilitated prayer ministries, and launched women's ministries. She has also been a speaker through other media such as streaming tv, radio, and social media.

She is also a U.S. Army veteran who served from 2001 to 2016, with two deployments alongside her husband, to whom she has been married since 2004. Prophetess Shearer and her husband Shaun have two children.

Instagram: fervently.creations
Clubhouse: Prophetess Tish Shearer
Facebook: Tish Shearer
Website www.ferventlycreations.com
Email ferventlycreations@gmail.com

Choose Your Best Life
By Carolyn Brooks-Collins

What life are you choosing to live? Yes, you heard me correctly; what life are YOU choosing to live? I say that because you have the power to take control of your life and your destiny. I know every person's life is complex, as we are the cumulative effect of all the experiences we've gone through, both good and bad. However, I believe no matter your age, or past experiences, you can still accomplish your dreams and live life on your terms. You have the power to live victoriously, and to thrive, no matter where you are in life, no matter what has occurred up to this point, and regardless of what others think. Ralph Waldo Emerson once said, "The only person you are destined to become is the person YOU decide to be."

Live the life you love! That seems so easy to say now, but that wasn't always the case. It was such a foreign concept for me to grasp. I thought it was a luxury I couldn't afford, that only wealthy people who didn't have to worry about their finances could live a life they loved. I lived a narrowly focused life, living to meet my family's needs and, quite honestly, meeting the expectations of others versus even allowing myself to envision what I wanted. When I did stop and wonder about living a different life, I was fearful and riddled with self-doubt. You know how fear can stop us at times. We are afraid of making a mistake, of being ridiculed for attempting to do something different, or perhaps we think we have waited too late to find our passions.

For 45 years, I worked in corporate spaces in the accounting field, working hard to climb the career ladder, but I was building the dreams of others versus my own. I made a career based on practical decisions versus having a passion for what I was doing. From the outside looking in, I was successful, but there was a yearning to do more or be more on the inside.

After seeing so many women give up on life after a specific age, not get ahead in their careers due to sexism, lack of guidance or a mentor, and making bad financial decisions due to a lack of resources and information, I knew I wanted to help other women find their voice, but fear still held me captive! I believed I didn't have enough experience to coach someone to change their life or even have someone listen to me. I even heard this from others, "Your life has been perfect, so how can you understand someone's journey?" Quite honestly, I embraced this thought until recently. I realized the phrase, "I don't look like what I've been through," applied to me.

It took finding a small plaque in my storage area to remind me of the things I have overcome. The plaque, purchased at a flea market in 1982, contained a quote by Camus: *"In the midst of winter, I finally learned that there was in me an invincible summer."* When I initially read it, I felt an inner strength and mental fortitude that I knew would see me through the winter I was experiencing.

Those words helped me through many "winters" in my life:

- When I purchased that plaque, I was in my early twenties and leaving a failed marriage. Three years into marriage with my HS/college boyfriend, I felt I had made a mistake. I also felt our relationship was a love that had succumbed to the pressure of constant questions – when are you getting married? Have you set a date yet? I also wondered deep inside if this shy nerdy girl who knew she was smart but didn't think she was pretty had based her decision on the fear that this was her only chance of getting married.

  To my dismay now, the thought of losing this boyfriend outweighed getting a free graduate education at the time. I know – that was crazy but true. So, we married, and from the outside looking in, we had the perfect marriage. Seemingly, very much alike, we had different goals in life, different ideas about marriage, and how you treated your spouse. It's funny but sad the number of things people don't discuss when getting married.

  Much to the dismay of my family and friends, I decided to leave. I was soon painted as the villain, scorned, and ostracized, especially by his family. Staying in that environment was not the future I wanted, and I decided to start over with a new job, in a new city, and alone. While I was scared, frightened even, I knew the invincible summer within would help me get through that winter.

- I remembered my inner strength and invincible summer as I encountered and survived another winter in my life – a second marriage that was not the best. As with any marriage, there were ups and downs, but I opted to stay in a marriage where I knew I wasn't loved. Again, I deferred my graduate school goals and opted to marry, thinking at age 31, I was getting older, and the chances of marriage may be less and less. Oh, how I would love to talk to this Carolyn and say, "Please put yourself first!"

  Again, I married someone whose concept of love, marriage, family, and children differed from mine. After years of thinking I might not be able to have children, I was pregnant with our son within two months! Our world was turned upside down by this life-changing experience. It was changed even more two years later with the birth of our daughter. I will sum this up by saying my "miracle baby" pregnancies were not filled with the blissful moments shown in movies and TV.

  During our 20 years of marriage, my husband grew into fatherhood and became proud of all three of his children. However, it was a long 20-year period, and I realize now everyone would have been better off had I decided to put myself, my peace of mind, and my mental health first! However, I didn't have the courage (or presence of mind?) to do that. Perhaps at the time, I even felt it would be selfish to focus on myself and my needs.

- My winters continued as I had to help my husband through the worst period of his life as he battled lung cancer for over 18 months from 2004 to 2006. I decided to put aside all the feelings and past hurts of our marriage and help him to the best of my ability. I knew I had to be strong for our three children, who were in high school and college, and the oldest had started his career. It was difficult as my husband was not the best patient, and I admittedly was not the best caregiver. It broke our family's heart when he opted to stop chemo treatments even though other trials were available. I accept that we each have the right to choose how we die but watching him was difficult during the last six months as the cancer spread and his life became smaller and smaller.

- I felt summer was upon me when I joined a new company shortly after my husband's death, but three years later, when I was down-sized, I realized then the winters would continue to come, but we need to learn to weather the storm, or even dance in the rain. I was one of 50 people who had to find a new position when the department was outsourced. I applied for every position offered but didn't know the results until an HR representative handed me an envelope that would tell me whether I had a job or would hit the streets looking for a job that following Monday.

I did get a new position, relocated to a new city, and worked in a new environment for three years. I landed on my feet and made the most of it, even finally earning my MBA. However, that sense of having someone control my life was one that I never wanted to experience again. I knew then that I needed to take control of my life.

Ladies and gentlemen, we have all had winters in our lives, and they may continue. However, you must believe that you have an invincible summer in you despite how blizzardy the winters may be. I want you to know you can overcome anything you have been through. You have a choice in how you live your life.

In late 2020, at the age of 66, I chose to start living my life expectantly, stop focusing on the past and focus on the future story of my life. I decided it was time for me to have an impact on the world using my voice. I invested in myself and took acting, speaking, coaching, and writing classes and training. I started reading books that helped me change my attitude about who I was and what I could accomplish. I started thinking about how I wanted my life to be at the end, and I immersed myself in the life I wanted to live.

Finally, I live a new and different life, doing things I never thought I would do: Helping women take control of their lives personally, financially, and professionally. Though I know we are all on a journey and growth is a lifetime experience, I want to share these four steps that will at least get you started towards living a life from within, where you ignore everything external to you, where you are in control and choose the life you want:

1. Give yourself permission to put yourself first and take responsibility for your life! Invest in yourself and know that you, your goals, and your dreams matter. Know that you have permission to take control of your life and start building YOUR dreams versus the dreams of others.

2. Decide what you want to do, what type of life you want, and believe you can achieve it. Open your mind to new possibilities using your hidden gifts and talents. Write your goals down and repeat them daily. Have the faith that you can achieve anything you put your mind towards. As Bob Proctor said, "Faith and fear both demand that you believe in something you cannot see. Therefore, choose faith and believe in yourself".

3. Get started and be resilient – never give up on your goals and dreams. Don't worry about how you will achieve them for the "how" will be shown to you. The key is getting started. As my mentor, Les Brown, says, "you don't have to be great to get started, but you do have to get started to be great!"

4. Create a plan and work that plan. Take daily action and be accountable. Surround yourself with people going in the same direction as you. Get an accountability partner and a mentor to keep you motivated and on track.

I challenge you to rise above anything that has held you back from finding the life you truly love. I'm here to tell you that you can control your life and destiny. I have realized that I believe in myself and have done so, quietly, in little spurts perhaps, but moving steadily in that direction. What I didn't know earlier in my life and truly believe now is that maintaining a positive attitude and mindset about life will take you further than anything else. You have to know that your life is worth living, that you can accomplish anything you put your mind toward, and that when you focus on the positive things in your life, thankful for every day that you rise, grateful for your ability to serve others as well as yourself, that you can live a better life than you are living if not even your best life.

About Carolyn Brooks-Collins

Carolyn Brooks-Collins, CEO of M. Carolyn Brooks-Collins, LLC, is passionate about helping to empower women to take control of their lives, step into their purpose and become financially independent. She is the #1 best-selling author, a Certified speaker through the Les Brown Power Voice program, a financial life coach, and a CPA. She is also a graduate of the Proctor Gallagher Institute's "Thinking into

Results" program, under the coaching and leadership of Mr. Jon Talarico. Carolyn has over 25 years of diverse leadership and management experience and is a strong proponent of leadership development within organizations. She has spoken nationally and internationally on the topics of taking control of your life and your finances, overcoming your fears, and finding your purpose. She understands that due to life challenges and priorities, women may often make financial decisions that are not in their best interest. Carolyn encourages women to take control of their lives and follow their dreams, regardless of their age and past experiences. Everyone was born to do something specific with their lives, but sometimes they need a mentor and a guide.

Connect with Carolyn Brooks
www.carolynbrookscollins.com
Facebook www.facebook.com/MCarolynBrooksCollins.

Learning To Serve From Nothing
By Charisse Burton

How do you serve when you have no value and nothing to give, or that's what you believe? When you hear, "When people find out who you really are, they will leave you," regularly, you become empty. When you are told repeatedly, "You are not important, you see yourself with no value."

That was my reality.

Not only do you hide who you are, but everything about yourself. You build walls thick as cinder blocks and taller than you can see over so no one can get to you because it will hurt too much for them to "really get to know you and then leave you." It becomes a goal never to let anyone "see in" and never let anything out, so people won't get to know you or find whatever monster is buried inside that will make "people leave me."

As you can imagine, there are a myriad of problems with this belief system, not the least of which is you are not acknowledging your gifts. Of course, that doesn't seem like a problem because you don't recognize that you have any. The idea of offering yourself to serve means nothing to you. It's just one more area to protect.

I know differently now. Even though now I believe I am powerful beyond words, I didn't start here. It's been a very long journey and one I'm still traveling.

How do you serve when you were belittled, forgotten, and abused throughout your childhood? How do you serve when from that abusive home, you were placed into a children's home? How do you serve when placed back in that abusive home? How do you serve when the childhood you lived ended with you as a teenage runaway? How do you find your way to serving someone else when your only purpose up to this point was to protect yourself?

The answer...I have no idea. I was in self-preservation mode for 18 years. I didn't think about serving. When I did, I was still convinced I had no purpose, that I had nothing to offer.

How does that change? How do you serve when you have no gifts, value, or purpose in your mind?

GOD.

You focus on healing. You focus on how God protected you throughout that crazy childhood. You focus on every place you can remember where God showed up divinely, even when you didn't know it. The next step is believing once you make it a regular habit to focus on how He was and where He was with you growing up.

When I was 18, a car accident changed everything. I was babysitting for a doctor's family while the parents were away in New York. After taking the child to school the first day, I was instructed to take the mom's car and go by the clinic they owned. I was supposed to pick up cash for the week and then get her car washed.

      While in the parking lot of that clinic, as I backed out of the parking space, a voice said very clearly, "Put your seatbelt on." This was 1987, so it really wasn't a thing to wear your seatbelt every time you got in the car; plus, I didn't want to wrinkle my clothes. I remember that thought going through my head. So, I continued to back out. Persistently, the voice said again, "Put your seatbelt on." Again, I ignored it and was a little miffed. When I got to the parking lot's exit, about to turn onto the street, the voice came again. This time with much irritation, with an audible huff, I threw the car in park and put my seatbelt on, begrudgingly. I even tried to smooth my clothes under the belt so they wouldn't leave creases.

      I turned right out onto the street and continued to the stoplight ahead. It was at an intersection where there was an overpass. I was going straight. The light turned green, and I eased out and drove under the overpass. The next thing I remember is crashing metal and shattering glass. When the car stopped spinning, I was stunned and obviously in shock. I saw people running, but it was blurry. Covered in glass, with an aching head where I hit the side window, and with bruises already starting to appear from where the seatbelt held me in, I looked around to see what had just happened. A car coming off the freeway, going 65, ran the red light and had hit the back quarter panel of the car I was driving, causing it to spin and hit a telephone pole. The hood of the car that struck me was no longer flat. It resembled an upside down "V." The ambulances came. Sirens were going off from the multitude of police cars on the scene. I was taken to the hospital, still in shock.

No cuts. No concussion. No broken bones. The ONLY injuries were the significant bruises on my shoulder, hip, and along my torso, where the seatbelt restrained me and kept me from flying through the windshield.

That was a turning point in my life. Who was that voice that I ARGUED with about putting on my seatbelt?

GOD.

Why did He save me? THERE MUST BE SOMETHING IMPORTANT ABOUT ME. I MIGHT HAVE A PURPOSE.

That would be a battle for many more years.

I battled with myself over what to think and believe. My doubts and fears would tell me one thing, but my hope and the memory of that car wreck told me something different. Perhaps our biggest and most crucial battle is choosing what to think and believe.

In fact, the only thing in this life we can control is our thoughts.

Words and thoughts carry POWER. They hold more power than we can possibly imagine. That's exactly why we are told to "**take our thoughts captive**," 2 Cor. 10:5. We have the power to change our reality with the thoughts we allow to hold space in our brains.

I had to change my thoughts. I had to find a new truth.

When I lived as a prisoner of the "truth" that I had nothing to offer, that I had no value to give, I lived exactly that. I did not serve. I did not offer anything of myself or allow anyone to get close enough to know me. But when I chose to change that truth and believe in who God says I was created to be, my life changed. My family's life changed.

Did that happen overnight? Absolutely not. It took time. It was and still is a battle. It takes constant reminders of who God created me to be from the time "**He knit me together in my mother's womb**," Psalm 139.

To me, we serve with our whole life. Serving is about offering someone else support to grow. It's about giving value to another person to become better or feel safer. Serving is about standing in the gap for another person who needs an extra hand. I had to start believing in my value before I could give value to others. Some steps I took to actively pursue that growth were: seeking God in everything, reading anything that would point me back to the truth of who God said I was, listening to podcasts that did the same, and journaling on a regular basis.

"**When you seek Him with all your heart, then you will find Him.**" – Jer. 29:13

Another turning point for me was a dream. I was in Heaven, standing in a hallway outside a big room.

The room had double doors with small windows, high up on the doors, almost like waiting room doors in a hospital. I could see inside. So, I peeked. There were rows and rows of people, all dressed in white. That's when I knew I was in Heaven. The people were worshiping and praising Jesus. I couldn't believe it. It dawned on me suddenly, Jesus was in that room! There was so much joy in there that the space practically glowed as if there were thousands and thousands of twinkle lights! The entire room was white and pure and bathed in warmth.

I wanted to be in there so badly, but I knew I didn't belong. I stood outside peeking in, wishing there was some way I could be worthy enough to be in that room filled with complete joy and endless hope. Even if I could just stand in the back I would be grateful. Finally, I thought maybe I could sneak in without being noticed. I knelt down, gently cracked the door open as slowly as possible, and crawled in on my hands and knees. I gradually moved down the row, careful not to disturb anyone as I crawled to the end and sat on the floor next to the wall. It was the last row in the very back; surely, I wouldn't be noticed.

There I stayed, hunkered down on the floor, just soaking in the joy and silently hoping I would not be caught and asked to leave. Then, there was movement from the front of the room. It seemed like a slow wave had started. Jesus was moving through the crowd of people. "Oh, no!" I didn't know what to do. If I tried to leave now, I would only draw attention to myself. I became so afraid I couldn't move. I knew I had been caught. I knew I was just about to be thrown out of a worship room in Heaven, maybe out of Heaven altogether! "Why couldn't I have just stayed out in the hall!?" Sweat started to run down the sides of my face. The palms of my hands were so damp with fear that they dampened the sides of my shirt that I had grabbed to cover my face.

Jesus kept walking. He was getting closer and closer to the back row. I was in the corner kneeling down, doing everything I could to disappear into the floor! I was sick to my stomach with nerves. He is going to see me! Jesus was going to see ME. All of Me.
Jesus came to the back row, turned, and started making His way in my direction. I was ready to throw up. I had nothing to hide myself. I was totally bare to Him. He saw me.
Jesus reached the end of the row where I was. I thought to myself, "here it comes." Tears of fear were streaming down my face. "He, JESUS Himself, is going to ask me to leave because I did not belong." Sweat dripped down my back. I buried my face in my pulled-up knees. I couldn't bear to see the disapproval I believed was coming.

Just then, Jesus knelt down in front of me. He gently put his nail scarred hands on either side of my face and raised it until my eyes met His gaze. With his finger, Jesus gently wiped my tears. He held my face in His hands and stared straight into them. At that moment, I was the ONLY ONE in that room. With His hands still holding my face, with His eyes glued to mine,

He stood raising me with him. As we stood there at that moment, I realized I was dressed all in white.

He didn't say anything. We stood there. At that moment, I knew beyond a doubt that I belonged. Then He took my hand and walked me down the row and up the aisle to the front of the room. Jesus turned me around as though presenting me to the rest of Heaven. There I stood, dressed in a beautiful flowing white gown now with a crystal crown.

I knew I had more value than I possibly could imagine.

I also knew this is how God created **ALL** of us to be seen. We are all created with more value than we could ever understand. The power of serving is to symbolically hold someone else's face in our hands and turn it towards Jesus.

CHARISSE BURTON

About Charisse Burton

Words have power.

No one knows that better or uses words more strategically than CHARISSE BURTON.

Charisse is a Business Strategy & Messaging Coach and Entrepreneur with over 18 yrs of experience. She is a content specialist, passionate motivator, messaging authority in her field, sage strategist, and founder of LIVE YOUR CHOSEN LIFE, LLC. Business

Coaching. Charisse is a veteran sales professional and runs a very profitable training program for sales-based business owners alongside her primary coaching practice. She is also the founder of The CLIENT ATTRACTION ACADEMY.

Charisse has spent many years both as an entrepreneur and training female entrepreneurs to reach their dream goals. She was a top leader in a 3-billion-dollar international company where her mission was to empower women to step out of the false belief they had adopted about who they are and into who God created them to be.
Her unique skills in building strategy, blended with her gift of creating relationships and developing response-driven messaging, make her outstanding in her field.

For the past year, Charisse has led a Mastermind program she co-founded for women to develop business strategies, increase their clarity, and sharpen their focus. She also leads a sales training program for female entrepreneurs. In addition, Charisse recently launched a NEW PROGRAM, The CLIENT ATTRACTION ACADEMY. This is a hybrid high-touch program to support businesswomen in identifying and removing any attraction blocks keeping them from connecting with their ideal clients. Then, create a plan to attract those dream clients organically and build predictable dream income. Charisse still finds it very important to hold space for those who need specific sessions. Therefore, she keeps a roster working with individual clients.

Charisse lives by two concepts that have supported her throughout her life. #1 on Charisse's vision board and the most important concept for her is to constantly work on becoming who God created her to be while helping others do the same. "You can do all things through Christ," is the scripture that has allowed her the strength to choose growth through all the obstacles she encountered in her "colorful childhood," as she refers to it. Most importantly, in all things, she is living a life that uses every gift God has given her to empower and bless other women.

The next concept that Charisse lives by is, "When you will work like no one else will for two years, you will be able to live like no one else can for the rest of your life," has been the foundation of keeping her focused in moving forward. This ties directly into living with freedom and providing her family experiences, which is #2 on her vision board.

When Charisse is not coaching, building strategies with clients, or supporting them in creating content attracting posts, she loves traveling and spending time with family. She is married to the love of her life, Andrew Burton, and the mom of four sons and three fur babies. Together their grown sons are each making their own significant impact in the world. Charisse and Andy are members of their church, where they play a role in marriage ministry. She is a trusted friend, a gifted encourager, and an asset to anyone who knows her.

Charisse Burton, LOVER OF GOD. WIFE. MOM. BUSINESS COACH. MOTIVATOR. STRATEGIST. WRITER.

LOVER OF WORDS. TRAVELER. SUPPORTER OF WOMEN.

cb.chosencoaching@gmail.com
www.facebook.com/charisseburtoncoach
www.instagram.com/charisse_burton
www.charisseburton.com

Stop functioning – start dancing through your life and live your dreams!
By Ellen Wulfert

It was the last day before the half-term holidays, the day I would have had to hand out the half-term certificates to my students. I was on my way to school early in the morning, so luckily, not many people were on the streets. My car was already doing strange things, and the lights of the instruments were blinking. Crazy enough, I thought, *"Today is an important day for my students – I have to go to school no matter what. My students and the headteacher are relying on me!"*

All of a sudden, the hands of the speedometer were spinning like crazy, I didn't even know how fast I was driving, and the lights had stopped working, too. While I was still thinking, *"But I must get to school somehow!"* my steering wheel blocked completely, and I couldn't do anything anymore - I lost control of my car and life.

While screaming and stepping on the brakes and holding on to the steering wheel, many thoughts crossed my mind, like, *"That's it?! What will happen to my son when I am not here anymore? Will I not see and help him grow up? How will I come out of this accident? Will I survive? Will I still be able to walk or dance? What about my plans and dreams? What about my vision? Will the graveyard rob me of all my dreams and potentials that I had always postponed?"*

Pictures of my teenage son crossed my mind in the seconds while trying to stop my car, and thoughts of regret that I didn't spend more time with him. However, I drove straight into a ditch of a field and finally managed to stop the car. And there I was - I lived! I was hardly injured, and nobody else was hurt. It was so amazing! Up to this day, I am so grateful.

And with this gratitude for surviving without being injured, I decided that no matter how painful it was, I wasn't going to live another day, just functioning. Now I was ready to change the world for mothers and their children.

In the weeks after this accident, I came to the realization that I had been working so hard for so many years. In general, I had been functioning for others, not for myself or my heart's dreams. I grew into the habit of allowing work to take up most of my time and energy, regardless of the consequences of my health, my relationships and to my great regret even regardless of my only beloved son. However, with this accident I realized I was given a second chance not to repeat the cycle of my parents.

From that point, I chose to have the confidence to live differently. And that was not going to be easy because things happened to me, like growing up with a bipolar and suicidal mother and an unknowingly abusive father. But as I was graced to stay on this earth, I listened to the calling this time to use the rest of my life to make a difference. Now I was ignited to serve and bring my vision to life.

My vision and mission

Like Dr. Myles Munroe said, *"Rob The Graveyard Of Your Treasure (Potential)!"* My vision and mission are to empower millions of children and teenagers. In order to do this, I help their mothers and people who work with children to be positive and strong role models so they can positively impact the lives of our next generation. My goal and dream are to elevate mothers as well as children and teenagers to pursue the life of their dreams by sharing with them how to create a healthy and fit body as well as how to develop a positive and strong mindset so that our next generation already during their childhood and youth experience how to:

   -**FIND** out about their goals and dreams,
   -**FOCUS** on their strengths and develop their potential,
   -have **FAITH** in themselves as well as
   -**FOLLOW THROUGH** to fulfill their goals and dreams.

And through this, *to "Rob the cemetery from their talents, gifts, and dreams to live a life that outlives them!"* as my great mentor Les Brown often says.

I am helping mothers and children prevent them from going through so many valleys and years as I did and instead get to the top of their lives much sooner. So, allow me to share my story with you and my big **WHY** for my mission.

The Story of My Childhood and Youth

I grew up in a broken home. My mother was bipolar and suicidal. I even found her several times after trying to take her life. So, I felt I had to protect my mother from an early age while my father beat me up almost every day for many years. As a child, teenager, and young adult, my home life was suicide, depression, anger, and physical abuse. Crazy dysfunction was my regular. There was no being happy at home, because there was no happiness allowed.

In fact, when I came home from school or the gym, often, my dad was so mad that he would yell, insult, or beat me up. He would continually hit me in my face or behind my head most of the time. And I didn't even know why he hit me. He was just so angry most of the time, maybe because he gave up on his dreams when my mum was pregnant with me to be able to support us. Yes, almost daily for many years, he hit me so often and so hard that today I suffer from severe pains in my neck and shoulder, which these recurring traumas in my childhood have probably caused. So often, I felt so scared and my heart was beating so fast when he was coming for me to beat me up. Yet I always fought back, and I learned to just function. My dear mentor Les Brown says: *"If you fall, try to land on your back. If you can look up, you can get up."*

And that is what I did. I got up again and again. Yet, I often asked myself, *"Why does my mom not protect me?" "Why does my dad hate me so much?" "What is wrong with me?"*

When I found my mom after she had tried to take her life, I wondered, *"Why is she doing that to me?" "Why does she want to leave me alone?" "Why does my dad not comfort me but is so violent and hurtful instead?"* And slowly but surely, negative beliefs and a lack of self-confidence infiltrated my subconscious mind as a teenager.

I couldn't even sleep at night. I was afraid that my father would take advantage of my body in ways he did with my mom against her will. When she had been taken to the psychiatric clinic so many times, my father expected me to serve the family as she did, and I felt even more at his mercy. It was functioning and getting through the day since my childhood.

However, the one thing that my dad passed on to me was his sport. As soon as I could walk, he taught me how to do alpine skiing. At the age of four, I started my career as a gymnast, and at 16, I pursued my dream of becoming a dancer.

So, the gym was almost the only escape from the tragic family life I had. I used to train almost every day after school. While practicing, I taught myself to focus on my strengths and develop my willpower and potential. I utilized that so people didn't even know what was happening in my life. However, I was happy when I had those endorphins from exercise flow. I felt free. In fact, my best friend said once, when we danced. *"Ellen, if I didn't know you, I would not guess by any means what you are going through. When you dance, you look so happy as if nothing has happened."*

And I realized – Yes, dancing and exercising are like a healing for me. When I hear the music and start dancing, I can be free because I can be me. I am very grateful to my father for introducing me to the universe of sports because from early childhood, I have experienced that exercising lifts my energy and vibration. By focusing on practicing, I can forget everything around me. Not only did I learn to develop strong willpower, but also how to fight back and survive and keep physically and mentally fit up to this day in my life. So, physical exercise is a tool that has kept me going and dancing through the ups and downs of my life until today. And in combination with mindset work, this is a powerful tool I would love to share with you.

What I learned from my mother and am also very grateful for was her unconditional love, creativity, appreciation for the "simple things" in life, the animals and nature, and the drive to keep going no matter how bad things were.

To be able to forgive has been a long and challenging journey for me. Yet, I experienced that forgiveness is one, if not the primary key, to our healing process and to taking our power back. Forgiving is not forgetting, but as Les Browns says, *"Forgiveness is remembering without anger."*

However, while trying to get through the days by discipline and functioning even in my adulthood, I was not allowing myself to have time for myself, for friends, or for building a relationship ending up fighting to survive with my son as a single mother by functioning.

When this accident happened, I finally realized I had to stop functioning. This took me 30 years! For a long time, I was so angry about myself for not having the confidence and watching others with less expertise but more confidence living their dreams. Being angry or depressed wasn't doing anything but hurting me and my beloved son.

But now, in the car accident, I had this life-altering experience. I became ignited to change, serve, and bring my vision to life to empower kids, youth, mothers, and all who work with them, because I don't want any child or any mom to experience what we have been through.

My goal and dream are that children do not have to worry about their mothers. So, they can be children and live a happy childhood, being elevated and growing up to be happy, healthy, and strong adults, creating healthy and happy relationships and again empowering their own kids and creating a better world for our next generations. My mentor Les Brown always motivates me with his statement, *"It's not over until you win!"* which has become my mantra. No longer am I functioning. I have answered my life call. This is the real Ellen.

I have clarity now and know what I truly really want and do not want anymore. I am dancing through my life.

Please, learn from my mistakes. As Les Brown says, *"Mothers, honor yourself and your children by pursuing your dreams!"* Stop functioning and start dancing through your life. Live your dreams!

If this chapter is reaching you today, I can help you. I would love to share more important steps that I have been practicing until today that can help you realize and change much sooner than I did.

Please reach out to me to get your free steps or schedule a free session with me.

My name is **Ellen,**

Empower
Love
Live
Embrace
New possibilities!

About Ellen Wulfert

Global motivators are born with a sense of universal influence, bridging various gaps between adolescence and maturity, rebellion and grace, body and mind. Embodying this nature in unyielding measure; is the compassionate professional Ellen Wulfert.

Ellen Wulfert is a coach, multivariate educator, and creator of the **EWM-Empowering Winners Method**, a program focused on the physical and mental empowerment of both children and teens. Having spent more than 18 years as a German bi-lingual educator, Ellen's facilitation has helped many develop and create positive mindsets and gain a more profound sense of self-confidence in combination with learning a new language.

Her mantra is simple: She wills to empower women and others who work with children through the power of self-actualization, physical competence, and mental esteem.

In congruence with an outstanding commitment to professional excellence, Ellen holds sincere regard for various forms of education, achievement, and community involvement. Alongside her educational acumen in English and Physical Education, she holds certifications in Yoga, Dance, Zumba, Fitness instruction and more for children, women and pregnant women. No stranger to word-class achievement, Ellen has facilitated international workshops for those looking to enhance their propensity for education and physical enhancement in Trinidad and Tobago, Germany, America, and more. Her passion for serving goes beyond humanity, as Ellen spent two summers in Crete, Greece rescuing sea turtles as a youth volunteer.

Displaying proficiency in a myriad of vocations and service-based business-led, Ellen into a profound relationship with mentorship and personal coaching.

Having been taught by professional coaches and mentors like Les Brown, Bob Proctor, Jon Talarico, Tony Robbins, Dr. Pamela Henkel, Apostle Deborah Allen, Tanya Powell, choreographers and dance instructors like Marvin A. Smith, Milo Levell, just to name a few, as a fitness instructor, yogi, dance teacher and body-mindset-trainer Ellen has acquired quintessential skill sets; yielding her as one of the most impactful influencers of her time. She is a proud international graduate of world-renowned speaker Les Brown's "The Power Voice Academy," establishing her well-earned appellation as an international speaker, author, and coach.

Enthused with a vision to accompany women, mothers, and children on their life-long journey toward wholeness, Ellen is committed to her craft on an intrinsic level. When she is not out training, teaching, and shaping the world for the better, Ellen remains an asset to her local communal body and a loving member of her family and friendship circles.

Ellen Wulfert. Leader. Educator. Humanitarian.

Contact Ellen:

What's app: (0049) 151 548 40 138
Email: teamellenwulfert@gmail.com
Facebook:
http://www.facebook.com/ellen.wulfert.39
Instagram: ellen.wulfert

What Lit My Fire To Serve Life's Now Worth Living

By Crystal Swanigan

Have you asked yourself, "Am I living my purpose?" Life is more than your achievement, gratification, peace of mind, career, business, or family. What is most important is how you live your dash and what you do with your life between your birth date and death date. When we take our last breath, hopefully, you are not thinking about the size of your house, the type of car you own, the size of your business, the titles you carry, or the degree you hold; those things, my friend, will all be meaningless at the end of life. One of my favorite quotes is, "Learn by experience, but it does not have to be your experience."

Strive not to be like those having a life-changing struggle or chaos before deciding to simply obey God's purpose for your life. Have you ever realized that one situation can pull the trigger on your life's never-ending cycle of problems that could indeed alter the entire direction of your destiny? This chapter will share a portion of one of many redefining experiences in my life that instilled a few of life's lessons that are worth sharing to help as you discover and walk into your purpose.

After having a sudden tragic medical attack in 2007, my grave-stricken body began to shut down as a result of a horrific deadly diagnosis that killed my eldest brother, Dr. Timothy Dale McCoy, in 1999. With bloodshot swollen eyes, I was lying in ICU at Barnes Hospital; my dear husband, Harmon Swanigan, was holding my hand when the doctor leaned over my bed and looked into my eyes, and told me that I only had possibly three days to live at the rate that my body was shutting down, minute by minute as the doctors were testing.

The doctor explained that a fatal disease was now taking over my body, and there was nothing more he could do. I needed a miracle from God, and I needed it fast because all of the diagnoses told to me in 2007 were the same told to my older brother in 1999. Death was coming after me with a vengeance after having a heart attack shortly after arriving at the hospital.

I cried out, only able to whisper to God, "My God Save me! I am not ready to die!" At the time, I was a little older than 40 and not ready to die physically or spiritually. I thought to myself, "Oh Lord, what else can go wrong?"

Well, let me tell you, my urine had turned brown, and as I was next diagnosed with Kidney failure, my Kidneys had begun to shut down. The death angel attempted to stop by my room in the middle of the night. As I had stopped breathing, our daughter, Krista, heard me struggling and gasping for breath. She woke up and yelled for the nurse as she pushed the nurse's button frantically, "Help me! Help someone please!"

Several nurses, doctors, and specialists came running to resuscitate my breathing. My breathing capacity had fallen under 50%. I was then hooked to all sorts of tubes as the doctors prepared to connect me to the Life Support machine as soon as it became available as that machine was being located and rushed into my ICU room.

I was lying there, and my body became scorching hot, burning with fever, yet I was shivering cold as if I were in the middle of winter with single-digit temperatures. The nephrologist told me that I would be on kidney dialysis for the rest of my life. But as my diagnoses and treatment plan evolved day by day while doctors struggled to try to find the problem and adequately diagnose my medical situation.

A few days into my hospital stay, they began giving pheresis platelet transfusion treatments, receiving up to 209 bags of platelet transfusions with 22 treatments over the course of a few weeks of being hospitalized. Our son, Eric, rushed home from Florida to see his mother, not knowing if this was the last time seeing his mom as the clock was ticking with very little time as my assigned medical team would try various medications and treatments to reverse this death sentence attacking my lifeless body. This was the most horrific, fearful, and painful experience both physically and emotionally in my life, causing tears to roll down my face.

I could not talk, but I was able to whisper short prayers begging my God for mercy and healing as I lay lifeless in ICU for 11 days and then downgraded to a regular hospital room for four additional days, continuing to plead with God for mercy. My loving husband, Harmon, was by my side every day, praying and calling for intercessors, holding my hand. My husband, son, daughter, family, and I all rejoiced as God began giving me a life back into my body; God was actually healing me as I went on my way. We serve an amazing God that knows the buttons to push to change our lives for the good. I asked God, "Have I made the most out of my life by serving my purpose?"

I felt like Hezekiah as I turned my face to the wall in Barnes Hospital St. Peters in room 273, asking God to please allow more time to serve Him as I carry out my purpose and serve others. My entire near-death experience story and more life lessons will be shared about how our God is still a healer regardless of what your doctor is telling you will be written in my upcoming book. Everyone enjoys the favor of God in their lives. But your anointing draws the fire of the enemy. Through my healing and many other traumatic situations, I experienced a shift in my life and a new level of success in God, knowing that I am a target. When you know you have graduated to new levels with God, shots will be fired at you from the enemy. But remember, you have favor with God. God placed the right ingredients to add to your test and trials to take out of your wrong attitude's put in you what is necessary to shift your mindset to serve and walk into purpose.

Seven years after this medical attack, in 2014, I was blessed to serve in the most fulfilling role that God could grace upon a person, and that is to be the pastor's wife of an amazing congregation, Grace Apostolic Family Worship Center. God is phenomenal, allowing me to be consecrated as a 3rd generation pastor's wife, ready to serve. Just when I thought that was the ultimate honor; one year later, in 2015, God graced me to be voted by my peers of 52 churches pastor's wives as the 10th President of Pastor's wives and Pastor's Widow's Auxiliary for the Pentecostal Assemblies of the World, Inc., 12th Episcopal District of the Midwestern District Council—serving as the 10th President for the States of Missouri and Illinois developing, mentoring, coaching leading ladies. As an auxiliary leader, I led and organized the pastor's wives and pastor's widows to work and raised funds exceeding $15,000 plus the first year. We also served the community's needs, which was a historical experience for the leading ladies.

This chapter will allow me to share a few helpful tips from my humbling near death experience that will help you mold and alter your life as you develop and walk into your purpose:

First, I want to help you realize that you were created to add to life on Earth by serving others. Have you realized that you can make a difference in this world? One day God will compare how much time and energy we spent on ourselves compared with what we invested in serving people.

Second, God never wastes anything that you may have or experiences you have lived through. Please realize you have special abilities, interests, talents,
gifts, personalities, and life experiences because God intends to use these as tools
for his glory.

Third, as you develop and move forward in serving others, you must strive to be committed. Many people often associate commitment with their emotions. If they feel good, happy, or accepted by others, they will follow through on their commitments. True servants of God do not serve based on their emotions, but they work based on their character qualities aiming to please God. True commitment is often discovered in the midst of adversity. When we face adversity, confusion, division in servants, and persevere while tired or hungry through disappointments, we know that we are committed to the assignment. My beautiful mother, Dr. Norma McCoy, once said, "Adversity fosters commitments, and commitments to your purpose will ignite you to hard work and get results."

The more you work at something, the less likely you are to give up on it. Don't give up, grow up, toughen up, shut up, and then you will go up. Remember, giving up is not an option.

Finally, another one of my favorite quotes that is used to alter one's habits and improve your character is "The 7 Rules of Life," which can make a difference in your life and help you get to the table of opportunity and bring someone with you with ambition and big dreams:

1) Make peace with your past so that it doesn't disrupt your present. You and I must decide not to allow people in your past to rock your boat in the wrong direction.

2) Don't give up. If it does not work the first time, find another way to make it happen. There will be times when you have to do it, afraid. Did you realize that fear paralyzes your next move, mind, and motivation, which are usually derived from people's perspectives?

3) Time heals almost everything. So, give it time. Only you can determine the "it" that needs more time. Don't give your fire and passion away to people that do not deserve your attention. Do not give your power away.

4) No one is in charge of your happiness but you. When other people make you happy or make you unhappy, you have given your power over to the other person. Remember, you are right about every situation; it does not matter. Don't always fight to prove your point to be right.

5) Don't compare your life to others. Also, do not judge others. We do not know the journey of others.

6) Avoid negativity. As much as possible, avoid negative thoughts, avoid negative situations, and avoid negative people.

7) Pray for people and simply smile. There are a lot of situations going on in the world. Lots of hurt people.

What's next? I look forward to traveling on international mission trips for His glory and to help serve others. I desire to have a servant's heart not to think less of myself but rather to think of myself less and others more. Consider this, Jesus only lived 33 brief years with 3 ½ years working in His ministry, being the example that we should not focus on the duration of our life but embrace the donation that we contribute to others.

About Pastor Crystal J. Swanigan

Pastor Crystal J. Swanigan, also known as Lady Swanigan, was born and raised in St Louis, Missouri. Marriage for 42 years since the young age of 16. She is a mother of two and blessed with five grandchildren.

Pastor Swanigan is a graduate of Missouri Baptist University, where she holds a Bachelor of Science Degree in Leadership and Ministry.

Crystal has worked hard as an entrepreneur since 1992 as a licensed Missouri Insurance Producer Property & Casualty, Life, and Health. Since 2001 she has successively served the community as a Buyer and Seller Real Estate Agent.

Since 2014 Pastor Crystal Swanigan has led God's people as a visionary and administrator with her husband, District Elder Harmon Swanigan, the senior pastor of Grace Apostolic Family Worship Center.

In 1992 she was the founder and director of God of a Second Chance Ministry, whose motto is Mending Hearts and Homes. She created programs to bridge gaps for people needing to pivot as they rebounded into having a second chance at life.

For the past seven years, Lady Swanigan has served as President of the Pentecostal Assemblies of the World 12 Episcopal District Bishops Wives, Pastor Wives, Ministers Wives, and Ministers Widows as she and the executive officer and pastor's wives authored two published books.

Pastor Swanigan spearheaded, trained, developed, and equipped wives on every ministry level and provided support and encouragement to surviving widows.

Pastor Crystal J. Swanigan has 50 plus years of leadership as a business leader, entrepreneur, and ministry.

There are several ways to connect with Crystal by going to
FaceBook: Crystal McCoy Swanigan or SwaniganInspiration Facebook Live on Mondays at 9

PM, CST, **Instagram:** LadyCJSwan. Visit my website www.Swaniganinspiration.com for upcoming new book releases, private coaching opportunities, Monday through Saturday group prayer sessions, conference motivational sessions, keynote speaking engagements, and more. Every Sunday at 11 AM and on Wednesdays at 7 PM, the doors are always open for amazing worship and praise experience, Grace Apostolic Family Worship Center 11770 Seven Hills Dr. Florissant, MO 63033.

RACHANDA SMITH

Serve Well Thou Faithful Daughter
By Ra Chanda Smith

Ever since I was a child, I have believed in serving, sowing, and honoring people. It has been a part of me since the age of five. I never wanted to do things if my heart was not in them. I believed in doing things with clean hands, a pure heart, and good intentions. I thank God that I've always had it in my heart to serve people, whether it was home, school, or church. I did not mind being uncomfortable, stretched beyond my normal capacity, or molded into a greater version of myself. *John 13:34 says a new commandment I give unto you, That ye love one another; as I have loved you, that ye also love one another.*

One of my favorite servants in the Bible is Joseph. Genesis 37 through 46 is a testament to how he went from the pit to the palace, from being sold into slavery by his brothers and them telling their father he had been ripped apart by animals to him running away from Potiphar's wife after she tried to sleep with him. Yet, he refused, so then being thrown in the VIP section of jail with the Butler and the Baker, he was forgotten about for two additional years. When the famine occurred, his brothers came to the palace to get their food rations but had to go back and get their baby brother Benjamin. Joseph could have been petty, but in the end, he was able to see that his family was taken care of. *Genesis 47:5-6 says that "And Pharaoh spake unto Joseph, saying, Thy father and thy brethren are come unto thee: the land of Egypt is before thee; in the best of the land make thy father and brethren to dwell; in the land of Goshen let them dwell: and if thou knowest any men of activity among them, then make them rulers over my cattle."*

    Serving others is so important to me, and I try to instill it in my children as well. You see, I grew up in the GREAT AME Zion Church. The first pastor and first lady I had did not believe in benchwarmers, meaning they wanted every member to be active and serve in some shape, form, or fashion, not to mention in tithes and offering. I was taught to be a cheerful giver and a sower.

    So with that in mind, I served in the children's choir (from ages 5-12), the Youth Choir (from ages 13-18), and the Junior Usher Board (from ages 12-18). I was also an active member of Varrick's International Christian Youth Council (ages 15-18), and I held various titles while doing so, such as corresponding secretary, treasurer, chaplain, etc. I was proud, and I took such joy in the work I was doing in my local church, in my district, and on my conference levels. *Philippians 2:4 "Instead of each person watching out for their own good, watch out for what is better for others."*

    Missionary work was engraved deep in my heart. We would have all kinds of programs and contests to raise funds. We would collect personal hygiene items and food to make gift baskets for the homeless at different shelters and the nursing homes. During my senior year of high school, I had the opportunity to represent my church to be a contestant in our fruit tree queen pageant. I picked a fruit, put together a basket of that fruit, and dressed in the same color as that fruit. The goal was to raise as much money as possible, as that fruit, and the money would be used for overseas missionary purposes. *Hebrews 13:16 says "Don't forget to do good and to share what you have because God is pleased with these kinds of sacrifices."* I love how *Proverbs 19:17 says, "Those who are gracious to the poor lend to the Lord, and the Lord will fully repay them."*

Throughout my childhood and teenage years, I would serve as a representative for our church. I would be elected official to give the synopsis when we would return from the events or various youth trips we would go on. We would have these huge conferences and youth retreats.

We always had the option to choose the classes and sessions we wanted to participate in during the events based on our different gifts, talents, or interests. I always chose choir and other activities that would stretch me. They believed in cultivating and arming us with the proper tools and resources. It was always a joy to be able to travel with my church family. I made so many friends just through traveling all over the United States with our conference area that I'm still connected to so many people.

In High School, I served in my community as a member of our Army JROTC program. I served on our

Drill Team and our Battalion Staff. I took pride in the impartation and cultivation of the next Battalions that followed me and the rest of the Staff I served with. I was proud to participate in drill competitions and community events, like parades or clean-up events. We even had a mentoring program with one of the Elementary Schools. We were each assigned a student to mentor and help steer us in the right direction.

These times taught me the true meaning of leadership and helped me lay the foundation of my own principles, morals, discipline, and values. I was very protective of my cadets and the students I mentored. I was proud to watch them graduate and go on and succeed in life. This really helped cultivate me as a mother years later. "When I stepped into Entrepreneurship, I began to see my business as a ministry itself. I am so passionate about helping women cultivate their gifts and talents and be able to help them monetize them. At first, I started with just doing coaching and virtual admin services to help my clients reach their goals faster, obtain their LLCs, obtain their EINs, and provide education on their business structure.

Then as I began to grow in my faith, I began to shift as time progressed. Now I offer Author Coaching and Book Publishing as services. In Habakkuk 2: 2-3 KJV, it says *2-And the LORD answered me, and said, Write the vision, and make it plain upon tables, that he may run that readeth it. 3 For the vision is yet for an appointed time, but at the end, it shall speak, and not lie: though it tarry, wait for it; because it will surely come, it will not tarry.* We have to truly be about our father's business in this season. Do you understand what that means? You have to write the vision God has given you and make it so plain that a child can execute it with excellence. Don't over complicate the process. Have a servant's heart. Keep your hands to the plow. Be a good steward of the things that God gives to you and the people. Serve God, your family, your community, and others.

I'm grateful for the hard times I had. I continued to sow into others. I continued to honor my leaders. I continued to Praise God in advance. I remember being on food stamps, and I would pay for the other person's items behind me. It was times I didn't know how I was going to pay my bills, but God allowed me to stretch the little I had. Sometimes I would look up, and I would still have that little bit I was holding on to. *Matthew 25:44-45 says, "Then they will reply, 'Lord, when did we see you hungry or thirsty or a stranger or naked or sick or in prison and didn't do anything to help you?' Then he will answer, 'I assure you that when you haven't done it for one of the least of these, you haven't done it for me."* This just reminds me that what you make happen for others, God will REMEMBER and make it happen for YOU!!

Everyone wants a title, but the greatest reward is just being a servant. **Matthew 25:21 - master replied, 'Well done, good and faithful servant! You have been faithful with a few things; I will put you in charge of many things. Come and share your master's happiness!'** At the end of the day, when this life is over, we have to give an account for how we used our time and how we treated others, **ESPECIALLY** the poor and the needy. You never know when you could be entertaining an angel in disguise. Treat people nice and serve well.

About RaChanda Smith

She was born on December 3rd, in Fort Rucker, AL, and is 30 years young. She is a native of Ozark, AL. She is the Mom of three- Reilyn (10), Bartees (4), and Jeremiah (2), a Domestic Violence Overcomer who co-founded a nonprofit called "Love Beyond," a co-author of "Love Beyond," (both of which she released with her co-founders Jakita, Michelle, and Katrishka). She is also the Self-Published Author of "Affirmations for the Broken Soul," A Business Strategist, Certified Life Coach, and so much more. She is passionate about helping the "Millennial Woman" grow and glow inside out and from head to toe. "Once you conquer your mindset, you can birth your businesses, break generational curses, and begin to create Generational Wealth."

Connect with RaChanda:

Website: http://chandasconsulting.com/

"You Matter!"
~ A Moment Between Lovers ~
by Danielle Bennett

It is life-altering the stories we believe from our upbringing and life events and how they shape our thought patterns and lives. "I don't matter" is the story I subconsciously believed since childhood. "I don't have a voice; I don't fit in anywhere." These are the narratives of my life that have traveled with me over my hills and valleys, leading me through darkness, violence, abuse, broken relationships, and a life that, while often on the right track, also came off in spectacular brokenness and traumatic heartbreak for my children and me.

These are life-destroying lies! I don't matter; I have no voice, and I don't fit anywhere. Astonishingly, I didn't realize this was what I believed! I didn't know my own narrative. If you had asked me if I thought these things were true, I would have said no; I know they're not true! This was not what I consciously thought; this was programming within my core, woven deeply into my subconscious and out of conscious thought. I knew I thought poorly of myself and my abilities, but I didn't know I believed that I didn't matter.

A few months ago, finding inner refuge for a moment in a battle-torn sea and taking a breath, I reflected on my life. Pondering the darkest moments when I know things could have gotten a lot worse, but for the grace of God. I know God has saved me and my children from moments in life of more suffering, let alone all the times I don't know about. Thanking God for his ceaseless strong arms and mercy and feeling them embrace me here. I saw how it has been through life's darkest seasons that I have experienced times of closest intimacy with him. I have learned His character in the darkest nights, fallen deeper in love with Him, gained insight, and grown in maturity. These gleanings are my life's treasures, precious beyond value to me, my desired jewels adorning my head and heart.

Startled by the treasure of suffering, I found myself offering thanks and honour for pain so deep I didn't think I would survive at the time. I would have wanted to attack anyone who, at the time, said this pain was for my own good. I could not bear it. Yet here, in this intimate moment, moved beyond words, realizations of God's tenderness and staying mercies washed over me, in his allowing me to pay the cost to find the treasure he knew I would value above any price, hidden and found only through the path of suffering. Selah.

I know how much I suffer when my children suffer, it is unbearable for me; I want to transfer their suffering instantly to myself so that I can go through it for them. Yet all I can do is go through it with them, hold their hand, climb down into the pit beside them and hold them. To impart my wisdom and insight when they ask me for it and to be there for them anyway when they don't. To be there for them in their unwise choices and when things fall apart. Oh, it would be far less painful for me to endure it myself instead of them. However, if I did this, how then would their roots push down deeper through rock and soil, probing for nourishment to strengthen and sustain them for life?

Like us, God would rather we didn't suffer, but for the treasure, we will find only through the pain; He chooses instead to go down into it with us, weeping over us, barricading us from worse evils in the darkest places. Guiding us towards the light, ever offering His strong arms and wisdom whether we take them or not, carrying us into our breakthroughs.

Slumped in a heap with immense gratitude heaving through my body, in uninhibited weeping, humbled to nothing, and in groanings without words, I poured out before my God and Saviour. Moved with awe, feeling every part of my humanity and His Godship, I tumbled into stillness and sat with Him wrapped around me. My heart moaned more than whispered its desire, "God, how can I make your dreams come true? What did you dream of when you first dreamed of me? How can I make that come true?" It was an unforgettably tender moment we shared—two parents, two children, God and beloved.

The next day I was talking with my sister on the phone. I don't remember what we were talking about, but it was anything and everything, and she said to me,

"Danielle, you need to write your story; you should be part of this book!"

This time, instead of saying, "No," as I had several times already, I said, "OK." Which I don't do. I don't create situations to put myself forward or step out of my cherished anonymity. I'm hermit-like, and I, like Shrek, like it that way. Surely, however, this would be a reasonably simple process, creating in an embracing group environment. I already enjoy writing; no one can see me, it's just a chapter in a book, and well, it's about God, not me anyway, so the spotlight's His not mine! Oh, to quell my fears. Things didn't calm down at this juncture; they got more shaken up, thrown around, smashed about and, like a volcanic eruption, hurled change in every direction within me!

In asking God for HIS dream, I had not considered how it might confront my learned, self-protecting ways. I had not considered anything at all. It was not premeditated; it was a surrender response to love. God's response to my surrender was to turn first His spotlight on what had been lurking out of my sight all my life, had choked me at every opportunity and kept me stunted and distorted in its prison of lies. In a moment, like a flash, He snatched out the lie of "I don't matter" and shone in His Truth, flooding my being with, "Danielle, you matter!"

It landed like an atom bomb inside me, flooring everything I knew. Only then, in the light of truth, could I, for the first time, detect the displaced lie torn out of my core.

I was flailing in a wilderness, confronted and stunned. It felt like I'd just been ejected from my own home and was suddenly uncovered, unprepared, and on a battlefield without warning, not knowing how to defend myself. 'Home' no longer felt like the safe haven it always had, but still, it was more familiar than being out here! Perhaps I could just crawl back in or curl up here on the back porch and go back to my old patterns. I could just keep really quiet so no one would notice me, or I could poke my foot forward a bit and take a step into the 'Unknown' and crane my head out to see a little further; then, if the coast is clear, take another step and take a look, and another, and another.

I was literally frozen between a new reality and an old familiarity, wondering what had just happened and how I got there. My deep inner fears and life patterns had been abruptly exposed and revealed to me for the first time. HEEEEELLP!!! I was out of my depth, flitting between panic and self-counsel that this is not about me; it's about God's will, plans, dreams, and what he has to say through this vessel. Well outside of my comfort zone, with my head talk, screaming to the tune of, "Aaaaaaarrrrrgggghhhhh!!!!! Run! Retreat! What's the point? Why write? Why change? I have nothing worthwhile to say! I keep my head down, I take care of my family, I mind my own business, and everyone else should just do the same! God's dreams?! What was I thinking?!!! I wasn't thinking...

It was a watershed moment. Here and now, I was being held to the flame. Was this really my heart's desire, or was it just fluffy sentiment in a moment of gratitude? Faced with a fiery furnace, the questions arose, "What do I value most? What God thinks and therefore has a plan for? Or my fears and my reputation? Do I have a backbone or just some nice intentions that cower and melt when the heat's turned up?

It is enlightening to face yourself in a moment like this—a swap; your relationship with God, for your fears. I had the choice to step into what God wanted, releasing me out of the prison that had held me all these years, or I could remain stuck. The choice was mine.

So much was going on inside me; I wrote it down to make sense of it. This is what I wrote:

THE LIE **I don't matter / I am unimportant**	**THE TRUTH** **I matter / I am important**
What I didn't know I believed... I don't deserve respect I will always struggle I only just survive I don't have a voice	*What I now know...* People must respect me I have choices I can learn anything The world needs my voice

I won't amount to anything My thoughts are irrelevant I don't make friends My husband won't be faithful to me I'm not good enough Others can do that; I can't I have nothing to offer I'm scared Women don't like me I don't know what I'm doing Just hide I don't have what it takes I am stupid	I can do anything I set my mind to. My thoughts matter; I can be anything I can make friends My husband will be faithful to me I am good at what I do; I do my best I can do that My offerings inspire people I chose faith, not fear I am a friend to women I have clarity of mind I speak my mind with ease I am enough I am smart

I have lived my 49 years believing the left-hand column, and destructive relationships, underachievement, and brokenness have ravaged my life. Yes, I am a lover of God; however, that doesn't magically make life perfectly landscaped and tidily proportioned within neat fences. It can be as torn up and rambling as mine and more. Being a lover of God also doesn't mean we suddenly become smart, lose all our 'baggage,' and become perfect little souls and bodies. As Wisdom said in the movie "The Shack," "There is no guarantee of a pain-free life." We are all in this life together, and we get to choose how we walk through the working-it-out processes. If any of the above rings true in any way or season for you, or you find yourself in a Watershed moment; this is what I've found so far on this journey.

Everything's changed. Everything's affected. Everything's challenged. I experience newness and wonder, like has the sky always been this blue? Have lilies always smelt this good? I have resolved to embrace the conflict my new decisions are creating, and I like it. I like the quiet inner strength that sits between my shoulders now, drawing them back with ease and simple gratitude, not bowing out in fear and retreat. New thoughts are occurring and affect everyone around me, my children, family, and others. My choices create change; how wonderful!

You and I matter. Each of us is of great value and importance and created through the unimaginable dreams of God. The world needs our contribution. I am only just awakening to the wonder of this and how simplistic and freeing it is. We can each make God's dreams come true if we want to, switching our agenda for His and stepping into the Unknown.

The catalyst for this life change was born out of the intimacies of a Lovers moment between God and beloved. God, holding me in His hands, me, His created being, moved beyond words to moans and surrender, so moved by the depths of His love's probing in my life through His relentlessly selfless strength and deeply tender mercies.

Oh, the inexplicable treasures of sitting in intimacy with our first love, the lover of our souls, laying in his stream of Living Water, drinking him in, our Source.

I am walking in the same life garden, sailing the same stormy seas, but with new eyes, seeing in the tender light of a golden sunrise the garden of Eden planted within me. You are His dream come true, too, walking in your own golden sunrise lighting up the garden of Eden within you. Let's walk intimately with Him in our Garden and seat him above all others, our first love, our Beloved, our Source.

About Danielle Bennett

The approbation of self begins with sagacious guides who have mastered their own paths of personal authenticity. Living this ethic by example; is the compassionate professional Danielle Bennett.

Danielle Bennett is an instructor, wellness advocate, and CEO and founder of **"You Matter**

Breath & Movement," a multifaceted faith-based physical practice specializing in the overall eudemonia of many. Having experienced success as a certified Yoga Fitness Trainer, she hopes to assist the global community with the essentials necessary to take care of themselves mentally, spiritually, and physically.

Her mantra is simple: She exists to make God's dream come true through the gifts he has given her and to share those gifts with the world. Alongside an amazing propensity for excellence, Danielle shares sincere regard for humanity, faith, and communal involvement. Through her practice, she intends to service a local women's refuge in her community; in hopes that she can share the value of wellness with women. Living up to the standard of servanthood, Danielle lends a helping hand to orphans, mothers, and single women, striving against the various storms of life. Impressed greatly by the heroic acts of Christ, Danielle understands servitude as an uncompromising commitment to her unyielding faith.

When Danielle is not out guiding others in the journey to self-actualization, she is a quintessential asset to her local community and a loving member of her family and friendship circles.

Danielle Bennett. Instructor. Advocate. Humanitarian.
www.instagram.com/danigypsy6
www.facebook.com/profile.php?id=100073718507379

Power to Laugh
By Dr. Clarice Howard

Hey, did you hear the one about the man and his wife, along with his mother-in-law, that traveled from the United States to Jerusalem for vacation? Unfortunately, his mother-in-law died there in Jerusalem. The local Funeral director gave his condolences and told the grieving son-in-law that it would cost six thousand dollars to ship his mother-in-law's body back to the U.S. However, I can take care of the burial here in Jerusalem at no cost. The son-in-law thought about The generous offer, but he declined. The funeral director asked, "Are you sure? You could save six thousand dollars. Wow, you must love your mother-in-law a lot to spend six thousand!"

The son-in-law said, "Well, thanks, but I heard a rumor that someone rose from the dead over here in Jerusalem after three days, and I just don't want to take a chance. So, send my mother-in-law back to the U.S., PLEASE!"

Life Was Good And A Barrel of Laughs

I was reared in a humorous family where we kidded each other constantly, especially when my Daddy was home. I'm proud to say, my Father, along with Former Supreme Justice Thurgood Marshall and former San Francisco Mayer Willie Brown, are descents of Pullman Porters. Pullman Porters were men hired to work on the sleeping and dining cars. Shortly after the Civil War, George Pullman recruited only Black men, many of whom were from former slave states, to work on his trains to carry passengers', Baggage, shine shoes, set up and maintain the sleeping berths and serve passengers. Although the porters were overworked, underpaid, and demeaned, my father kept his integrity and humor. He'd tell us jokes and stories of a few movie stars he saw, such as Clark Gable and others traveling across the U.S to promote their films. When Mama and us kids, My brother, and big sister, would pick daddy up from St Louis Union Station in our 1953 green Dodge, the jokes and laughter would start up. With my Daddy's paycheck, tips, and my mother's ingenuity, they could own three rooming houses renting out kitchenette apartments at fifteen dollars a week. Hey, life was good. I even got a quarter for my allowance.

The Curtain Comes Down

When I was eleven years old, Mama drove Daddy to the Veterans Hospital, but he never came out of there. He died there of an enlarged heart, I was told. At the funeral, I kept thinking, "This is

Some kind of a hoax."

But at eleven, I didn't dare ask. Mama was left with three kids, and the properties were difficult to maintain. Mama sold off two of the rental properties. Consequently, the Quarters allowance stopped; it was like my own little Wall Street Crash of 1929. What to do? I know – what all kids do, turn in Soda Pop bottles for a nickel a piece. Ha! Ha! The power of laughter kicks in. My own little enterprise. Despite the lack of new clothes, the only eerie thing was the fact the laughter stopped. My brother left home, and my big sister married her 6ft 7in high school sweetheart and then went away to the Army.

With Mama struggling to pay the bills, what does she do with a limited education? She does what a lot of women do. About six months after we buried Daddy, which I still think is an elaborate hoax, she marries one of the ministers from our church. After he dies, she marries again. The third husband bites the dust. Mama was an expert at being in her "Survival Mode." Mama passed away at 100 years old. I miss her.

Proverbs 17: 22 Laughter Is A Good Medicine, and I'm going to need a heavy dose

King Solomon was a very wise king. Laughter enhances your oxygen, stimulates your heart, and relieves stress. As a Pastor, I have encountered stressful stuff, like when my brother, who confesses to being an Atheist, had it in for me. Big time. He had been gone around fifteen years. No one knew his whereabouts. We assumed he was dead. I fasted and prayed for the Lord if he was alive and for his salvation and to see him. Hey, be careful what you pray for. Our mother, who had lived to be a hundred years old, died.

My brother came back to town with a vengeance looking for some sort of inheritance. There was none. Learning the house that mother lived in had long been sold only fueled his hatred, and I was his target. He offered one thousand dollars on Facebook to anyone that "Would do something to her, " a hit. Hey, this is no joke! Actually, I thought I was worth more than a thousand dollars; oh well, I guess that was his budget. It didn't work.

One Sunday morning at the church that started in my home, my dear brother picketed out and handed out derogatory flyers. When the police showed up, he informed the officers that he had a right to picket a church, which is true; however, he antagonized the officer until the officer responded, "Look buddy, you better move away from this lady's house, because as far as I'm concerned, I don't see no steeple on top of that house and that ain't no church; and if I put you in my squad car, you ain't gonna like it."

My brother left. I thanked the officer, went back inside, had a laugh, and continued to preach the Word. My brother shows up at our mother's funeral, where he sits on a pew and curses and swears at our mother as she lies in her beautiful pink-lined white coffin. By the way, I'm so glad I upgraded on her coffin because the blue one she had chosen in her burial plan reminded me of one of those foam coolers that you see at the liquor store for ice to take to a picnic.

Anyway, I had the funeral directors and deaconess escort him out of the church. In the limousine, as I rode to the graveyard, the Holy Spirit told me that my brother was at the cemetery. Sho'nuff, he was there ready to clown; but the men folk calmed him down and protected me. I really felt sorry for him. I laughed within myself and hoped that I had ordered enough chicken for the repast.

The Lord blessed our congregation to purchase a church building. So then came the bomb threats from guess who? The police brought out dogs to sniff for a bomb. They asked was my brother ever in the Army and did I think he had the potential to make a bomb. I don't know, but I do know he didn't have the potential to make a decent pitcher of Kool-Aid when we were kids. I'm glad the city doesn't bill for bringing those bombs sniffing dogs. That is not in the church budget.

Eventually, King Saul Gave Up Stalking David

It's been ten years since my last encounter with my brother, and when the dust cleared, *I'm still standing*, only by the grace of God. My brother suddenly stopped his roaring like A lion, threats and character assassinations. I heard he moved out of town. I don't know where that thorn went, and I don't care. Oh yea, and I've forgiven him. Yes, there were times when I was scared because of the stalking. The Restraining Order of the courts that I filed doesn't last forever; they expire. I still have copies of the derogatory flyers he passed out throughout the neighborhood.

I reminisce on the power of God's protection, the power of prayer, and the power of laughter in the times of the fiery trial, which is to try us as though some strange thing happened unto you, as Apostle Paul writes. Along with Jesus' teaching of the Sermon on the Mount, *Blessed are ye, when men shall revile you, and persecute you, and say all manner of evil against you falsely, for my sake. Rejoice And be exceeding glad: for great is your reward in heaven: for so persecuted they the prophets which were before you. No weapons formed against you shall prosper or be successful, daughter.*

I leave you with this, *"He who sits in the heavens shall laugh: The Lord shall hold them (the unrighteous) in derision. "* The Lord gave us the gift of humor and laughter, so don't waste it.

Thanks for reading my adventure. Hey, did you hear the one about the Easter donkey? Never mind, I'll tell ya next time.

Acknowledgments

I want to give Glory to God for filling me on a cold Friday night on January 1980 with the Holy Ghost. Wherefore, I experienced a radical life change through Jesus Christ and the Word of God.

I thank my now, Heavenly father and mother, Cleveland Carson and Missionary Helen Surzette Carson, for providing a Godly home full of humor.

I Thank my Adult Sunday School Mentor, the late Evangelist Mary Wood, for her advice to always watch the Leadership in the church and learn.

To Dr. Joe Crephas Bingham Sr. And Dr. Bettie Bingham for encouraging me to always reach for scholastic achievement. I still hear his encouraging words spoken on the sidewalk in front of Glad Tidings College West Belle location, "Sister Howard, someday, you're going to go far."

To my daughter Maureen Williams who provides me with a wealth of information and love.

I want to thank my brother in the Gospel, Bishop Earl Anthony, and Lady Linda Anthony for always being there, a truly divine connection. What can I say about Apostle Deborah Allen? Her motivation is to reach greatness by using the power and potential within us. We can soar like an eagle for Jesus Christ and the community.

Lastly, I want to acknowledge all those who will read my segment along with the other authors of this book. Love ya.

DR. CLARICE HOWARD

About Dr. Clarice Howard

Dr. Clarice Howard is blessed to be the founder and senior pastor of the Living Waters Church of God Fellowship, located in Saint Louis, MO. Dr. Howard, received her early Godly teaching from her mother, Missionary Helen Surzette Carson; and under the Pastorate of Bishop Austin Augustus Layne, Pastor of the Temple Church of Christ.

In 1980 Dr. Howard became a Holy Ghost filled on fire for the Lord Woman of God. In 1982, the Lord called her from 2 Timothy 4: 2 "Peach the Word." She has served on the Prison and Chemical Dependency Ministries, Director of V.B.S. President of the P.A.B Ushers, Camp counselor; and whatever her hands find to do, she does it with all of her might. She's the former host of the King's Kids radio broadcast. Mental Health advocate with Bridges to Recovery Programs Inc. Dr. Howard is the current secretary for the M.D.C. Advisory Board.

Dr. Clarice Howard earned her Bachelor's degree in Biblical Studies and was awarded Valedictorian of the class of 2006 from Glad Tidings College. She earned her Masters degree and Doctorate of Theology from Midwestern College of Theology. Glory to God!

Pastor Howard is a woman of prayer and has expressed its results. She is an effective communicator of the word of God, widely known for her practical and dynamic teaching style of wit and humor, which will motivate people of all ages to apply the timeless truths of scripture in our everyday lives.

Dr. Howard is happily married to Deacon Robert Howard. She is the mother of two adults daughters, six grandchildren, and four great-grandchildren.

Dr. Clarice Howard's motto is, "Don't Quit, Because The Best is Yet To Come."

Connect with Clarice
livingwaterscogf@yahoo.com
Facebook: Clarice Howard
Website: lwcogf.org
(314) 609 6309

From The Valley To The Mountain Top (Soaring)
By Joyce Kamau

"Consider it pure joy, my brothers and sisters, whenever you face trials of many kinds, because you know that the testing of your faith produces perseverance."

James 1:2-3

It's not easy to celebrate tough times. However, if there is ever a time when you must be brave, audacious, tenacious, and innovative, it is during the storms. Never ever give up.

The Molo Meadows

Growing up in the rural Kenyan highlands, I walked a six kilometres journey to school with no shoes and often in the biting morning dew. School mornings were challenging. However, the afternoon journey home was fun. We played along the way, enjoyed eating wild berries, and quenched our thirst with pure spring waters of the Molo meadows. I had a fantastic and memorable childhood.

In the little known Kambala primary school, I teamed up with two friends to showcase musical performances during special days at school. Lydia had moved from the city of Nairobi to live with her grandmother in Molo. Wendy had relocated to Kenya from the United States of America with her parents. Magìrì, the village girl, did not shy away from teaming up with the more exposed girls to make a powerful trio. I was determined to learn and embrace the opportunity and be the best that I could be.

Together we made great performances, winning accolades from teachers, parents, and students. My memorable performance was "He's got the whole world in His hands ." Looking back to my childhood through my career lens working in the international arena, I can attest that God has the whole world in His hands. Our destiny is always in His hands.

In academics excellence, Waweru, Nduati, and I showcased healthy competition. We alternated between the first, second, and third positions. We received many awards for excellence which I dedicated to my parents. I wasn't intimidated by the boys. I was determined to excel. Mathematics was my favourite subject, thanks to Mr. Kuria, *"toa mukono nje,"* as he was in students' circles.

Lessons from my parents

Growing up under my beloved mother's wings, I learnt the importance of courage and determination. My mother (Nyina wa Karimi) had no opportunity to go to school; nevertheless, she was a resourceful member of the Molo Dairy Board (the only woman at the time) in the late 80s and early 90s, a dedicated Deacon and a member of the Women's Guild at the Presbyterian Church in Molo.

She worked extremely hard as a small-scale farmer to raise eight of us while my dad worked in the city. She woke up early to milk her cows in time for the early morning milk collections and prepared our snacks for school, which included the yummy charcoal-roasted corn. It was a remarkable balance of responsibilities. She valued education and resolved to see all of us excel.

Meeting Protocols 101

As a member of the Molo Dairy Board, my mother was exposed to structured meetings. This was a skill she was keen to share and inculcate in the community. It was usual for us to hear her mention standard meeting terminologies often with a Kikuyu accent: agenda *("ajeda")*, matters arising *("mataraisini")*, minutes *("mīnīti")* A.O.B *("OB")*. She emphasized the power of showing up and making your voice heard. She travelled across the country for conferences and agriculture trade fairs. I remember her travels to Embu and Naivasha as she shared vividly her lived experiences. She inspired me at a young age. She taught me the value of integrity, hard work, determination, courage, speaking up, patience, perseverance, conflict resolution, gratitude, and strong faith in God. Her favourite scriptures are Philippians 4:4-5. *"Rejoice in the Lord always, I will say again: Rejoice! Let your gentleness be evident to all, the LORD is near."* The Beatitudes, in Matthew 5:9, was her conflict management guide. *"Blessed are the peacemakers, for they will be called sons of God. She was a servant leader per excellence. I'm forever grateful that my mother introduced us to God. God bless her soul."*

My dad taught me loyalty, diligence, sacrifice, patience, and giving with a cheerful heart. He was the firstborn in a large extended family. He belonged to the clan, he was responsible for his siblings and many cousins. He gave generously even his own clothing! He was loving, and valued education. He and was determined to give all his children an opportunity for the best possible education that he could afford.

Trusted hands

My dad was a trusted and loyal chauffeur of thirty years for the General Managers at Olympic Airways, regional offices in Nairobi, Kenya. He worked diligently and won the confidence of his bosses. Through his dedication and loyalty, one of his bosses entrusted him to travel with his children for summer holiday in his home country, Corfu, Greece.

Determination and courage were strong foundations in his driving career. He shared with us his experience taking his driving test under the strict colonial driving examiners. He was the only one who passed the test in a group of about twenty people. He recalled with satisfaction how the strict examiner was evidently impressed by his driving prowess.

Inspired by the values inculcated in me by my parents, I feel their presence every day as a parent and in my professional career.

Banking on Human Resources

In May 2011, in a Management publication by the Kenya Institute of Management, I was featured as Top Woman in an article titled "Banking on HR ." I was Head of HR in a commercial bank.

My career began as a humble bank clerk at Barclays Bank of Kenya. I was determined to excel in banking. I worked hard and ventured into the foreign exchange area, which many people avoided as it was considered challenging. This would open an opportunity to venture into Human Resources.

While on a Foreign exchange course at the staff training centre in Karen, Nairobi, a team from the UK headquarters was visiting. They visited the training room where I was making a presentation on a group activity. Impressed by my presentation skills and understanding of the subject matter, while giving feedback to the then Head of Training, Mrs. Janice Mwosa, they applauded her for a capable team, referring to my presentation only to be informed that I was a participant. They recommended that I join the team.

During the interviews, I recall Janice posing the question, "Where do you see yourself in three to five years?. Without hesitation, I responded, as Head of Training! I joined the Barclays Staff Training Centre in

Karen Nairobi as a Trainer at the age of twenty-six. My branch manager at the time reckoned that I was too young to be promoted!

I started on an exciting note. I loved training and consistently received positive feedback from participants. Unfortunately, this was not received well by some of the trainers. I remember Janice encouraging me with words that remain with me to this day. She said, "Joyce, whenever you find yourself facing such resentment, especially when good reports are received on you, know that you have something bigger than your critics."

Three years later, Mrs. Mwosa retired, and I was appointed Head of Training! She was the bearer of the good news.

When the dream is big, the odds don't matter. Always keep your eyes on the goal.

The Valley

Throughout my career, I have faced challenging situations. However, from 2018 to 2021 was my lowest moment.

Prior to this period, my star was shining. I had a very promising career in an international organisation. I embraced new responsibilities with diligence. I recall an impromptu assignment to hold fort as head of delegation on an important mission. With dignity, grace, and a high sense of duty, I effectively led the mission propelling me to the limelight. Sadly, this did don't go well with some colleagues; friends turned foes. I felt betrayed; I was disenfranchised from an opportunity for promotion and humiliated. I was emotionally depleted. It was a tough place to be in. I could have easily given up. "Anyone can give up; it's the easiest thing to do. But to hold it together when everyone else would understand if you fell apart is true strength "anonymous. I was comforted by Psalm 23:4. God was with me in the valley.

If it doesn't open, it's not your door. Be patient. "Patience is not the ability to wait, but to keep a good attitude while waiting," Joyce Meyer. Be hopeful in the Lord. "But those who hope in the Lord will renew their strength. They will soar on wings like eagles; they will run and not grow weary; they will walk and not be faint." Isaiah 40:31

While in the valley, believe in the possibilities. Take comfort knowing that God's power is made perfect in weakness. Difficult as it might be, remain steadfast, maintain high standards of excellence, living each day with dignity and integrity. As Michelle Obama noted, when they go low, we go high. Above all, trust in God. He knows the end from the beginning. He has good plans for you. Jeremiah 29:11. Draw strength from the lyrics of the song by Bill and Gloria Gaither that the God in the mountain is still the God in the valley. When things go wrong, He'll make them right.

Be Still

Let go and let God.

Psalm 46:10 encourages us to be calm during the storm acknowledging that God is fighting our battles. He orders the wind, and it obeys Him. Embrace a new mindset that shapes your worldview. "Once your mindset changes, everything on the outside will change along with it," Steve Maraboli. Embrace the mindset of a hero, not a victim; courage, not fear, abundance not scarcity, growth not fixed; agile, not rigid mindset to set you on a journey to the mountain top. You are more than a conqueror s.

Prayer changes things. Seek God. Even when you lack the words, be encouraged, knowing that the Holy Spirit Himself intercedes for you with groans that words cannot express. Romans 8:26-27.

Do not be a slave to fear. Stay strong, let your gentleness be evident to all, and the Lord will show up in the fullness of time. "Do not be anxious about anything, but in everything by prayer and petition with thanksgiving, present your requests to God. Philippians 4:6.

I'm grateful to my prayer warriors: my dear sister Nancy and my friends Mary, Grace, and Jane, and many others who uplifted me in prayer in their privacy. May God bless you exceedingly.

Be determined and hopeful. Dedicate yourself to a bigger course larger than yourself. Begin developing yourself, be intuitive. Discover the power within you. Finding value in life and mind coaching was meaningful to me while in the valley. I was on a mission to help individuals be the best they can be. Getting accreditation from the International Coaching Community, UK, was a significant milestone. Thanks to Joseph O'Connor. SOAR Coaching Solutions Limited was borne. I'm grateful to my cheerleaders of this big dream: my family (the quads), Sandra, Julie, Jane, Mwangi, Josephat, and Nyambura. Thank you, Sandra, and Julie, for giving me a coaching opportunity. I'm so proud of your success.

Commit yourself to being the best you can be. Continuous personal development is key to unlocking your full potential. Invest in it. Finding a source of inspiration during and beyond the storm renews your motivation. I draw a lot of inspiration from the example of our Lord and saviour Jesus Christ, the Word of God, my parents, Joel Osteen, Bob Proctor, Jon Talarico, Les Brown, Michelle Obama, Wangari Maathai, among others.

Restoration; Beauty for Ashes; A new song

Mourning lasts for the night, but joy comes in the morning. When the time is right, the LORD Himself will make it happen. Isaiah 60:22. God came through for me in an overwhelming way. He made a way in the desert for me. Streams began to flow in the wastelands. God did a new thing. It sprung up for me! He catapulted me from Lusaka, Zambia, to the iconic Malborough House in London, United Kingdom! He is an awesome God. I can attest to the words of Isaiah 64:4 and 1 Corinthians 2:9 that indeed no eye has seen, nor ear has heard, no mind has conceived what God has prepared for those who love Him. He did it for me; He can do it for you. Remain steadfast in Faith.

From the Molo meadows in Kenya to the Hertfordshire meadows in the United Kingdom, I'm blessed beyond measure. Indeed, the LORD is my shepherd; I shall not be in want. He makes me lie down in green pastures; he leads me beside quiet waters; he restores my soul. Surely goodness and love will follow me all the days of my life, and I will dwell in the house of the LORD forever.

Signed, Joyce Kamau

About Joyce Kamau

Joyce is a loving mother of two wonderful boys, a young adult, and a Teen.

She is a Human Resources professional, an International Certified Coach and a member of the International Coaching Community (UK).

She is passionate about helping individuals unlock their full potential and be the best they can be.

A co-founder of SOAR Coaching Solutions Limited, she is dedicated to providing goal-oriented leadership solutions through a journey of self-awareness and self-discovery.

Contact Joyce:

magiri@soarcoachingsolutions.com

Unleash Your Destiny
By Kelisha Worrell

Are you frustrated because you are working so hard, yet life seems to be giving you poor results? Let me help you ignite your fire and find the passion within yourself again. I am Keli Worrell, a #1 bestselling author, Television Show Host, Certified Les Brown Speaker, and founder of Destiny United Institute, a personal development coaching program. I specialize in helping women unlock their potential, breakthrough barriers, and change direction in their life forever. To learn more about how you can unlock your potential and go to the next level, go to www.kelishaworrell.com

Introducing Destiny Unleashed

Previous to developing the Destiny Unleashed program, I had a prestigious position with an organization, and my life was going nowhere. After I left my job, I decided it was time for me to reinvent my life and design one that I truly wanted to live. While reinventing my life, I wanted to create a **destination** that equips women with the support, tools, and resources to become successful entrepreneurs, creating an amazing life for them and their families.

"Destiny Unleashed" is a transformational program that helps women discover their gifts while exploring ways of maximizing their best selves to create a lifestyle experience, not just a getaway. It's a place where SOURCE meets SUBSTANCE to create SUCCESS STORIES.

Leaving my job to pursue my dreams was one of the best decisions I have ever made. It was scary, but it was also empowering. I realized that if I wanted something different in my life, I had to take action and create it for myself. And that is exactly what I set out to do.

There is an undeniable power that comes from creating your life by design. It's a mindset that sees beyond the current circumstances and limitations. It's the ability to let go of everything that's holding you back, including fear, doubt, and insecurity—empowering you to step into your greatness and create the life you want. When you live with this mindset, anything is possible. You become UNSTOPPABLE!

I have been there and understand what it's like to be full of struggle, ineffective, and miserable. I'm here to change that for you and help you get excellent results in whatever area you choose, from your health to your finances and relationships.

The thing that led me to create my coaching program is that I was tired of feeling stuck and frustrated—tired of waiting for someone else to give me permission to go after my dreams. So, I decided to lean towards faith, not fear, and create the life I knew was possible.

If you're tired of feeling stuck, write down I AM PROSPERITY on a small piece of paper. Keep this with you, and read it out loud daily. Your life will begin to transform.

Get Clear On Your Goal

The best way to design the life you've always wanted is to first get clear about what it looks and feels like. What are your passions? What are your values? Once you know that, start thinking about the different areas of your life and what you would like to change. Some people might want to travel more, learn a new skill, and make more money. It's up to you to figure out what you want and then start taking steps in the right direction. Remember, it's not about getting everything perfect all at once. It's about taking incremental steps every day that will get you closer and closer to your goal. Rome wasn't built in a day, and your business won't be successful overnight either. Just remember to stay focused and don't give up, no matter how hard things may seem at times.

Stay focused and set BIG WORTHY GOALS. When it comes to goal setting, many people make the mistake of thinking small. The problem with setting small goals is that people actually achieve them. They'll set a goal to save an extra $50 each month or to work out for 30 minutes three times a week. While there's nothing wrong with these goals, they likely won't result in massive changes in your life. If you want to see real progress, you need to start taking massive action on your goals.

There are many things you can do to set yourself up for success when moving towards achieving your goal. It's important to make sure you're moving towards something you really want and not settle for what you think you can have. A massive goal will push you to take action and achieve great things. It will also give you something to look forward to each day and keep that fire burning within you. If you feel excited and scared at the same time, it's most likely the right goal to set.

Les Brown says, "Most people fail in life not because they aim too high and miss, but because they aim too low and hit." Having a worthy target will keep you moving forward.

Another important step is to celebrate your successes along the way, no matter how small they may seem. Acknowledge your progress and reward yourself for your hard work. Ever wonder why the winners in life just keep getting great results and winning? It's because they program their mind to see success & you can too!

Your brain has a network of neurons called the RAS- (Reticular Activating System). This system is in charge of identifying what's most important to you and filters out the rest of the data coming into your mind from the outside world. Once you begin to program your mind to see success, your RAS will start to spot opportunities everywhere, and you, too, will begin to win!

I remember a time in my life when I wasn't winning; I felt like giving up. I have always been an extremely loving person all my life, but I was vulnerable to being mentally and emotionally abused in my former years because I wanted to see the genuine side of people and ignored all the red flags, so I continued showing them the bright side of life in hopes that they would one day change, I couldn't be further from the truth. I was manipulated, verbally, emotionally, and mentally abused. My life became more than I could control, and I had been living with a spirit of fear for many years.

I found myself in a place where I felt like everything was falling apart, and I knew I had hit rock bottom and didn't know where to turn next. If you are currently in this situation I want you to remember… there may be times in life when you won't know what will happen next and you can't control the situation; don't panic or get angry. Increase your efforts to progress and use your mind and not your emotions to protect yourself.

One day all that ended, and my spirit couldn't take the abuse anymore; I fell on the floor of my house, flooding the wood with tears as I cried profusely, gasping for air until my body gave out and had no more strength. It felt as though I died right there on the living room floor for a moment. With my face to the ground, I gasped for air, and with all the strength I could muster up, I whispered the words… "God Make Me Whole." After that day… I decided it was time for me to win.

Although you may have heard the myth that time heals all, I'm here to share with you that time heals no wounds but the (decision not to stay wounded does.) It's been said that "Wherever you are in life at this very moment, at some point in time, you made an appointment to be there."
DECISION is the ultimate power... it is your most valuable resource, and how you make your most important decisions could have a tremendous impact on the quality of your life.

Designing Your Destiny
When you decide to design your life, you get to choose everything. You get to choose the people you want to be around, the work you want to do, and the lifestyle you want to live. It's a very empowering way to live!
I am so passionate about helping women achieve their dreams that I created a space to do just that. The goal of my program is to provide women with the support, tools, and resources they need to become successful entrepreneurs. This is an amazing, life-changing opportunity. Here are a few tips to help you make the next step forward:

1. Believe in yourself. You are capable of anything you set your mind to.
2. Create a daily routine that will support you in achieving your goals.
3. Have a clear vision and purpose for your life. What is the BIGGEST goal you want to achieve?

4. Create a plan of action.
I know what it's like to live your life trying so hard to make things come together, but feel like you are being dragged by life circumstances. If this sounds like you, I want you to know that right now you have within you everything you need to be successful. You have the power within you to heal, make peace with your past and advance your life.

How to apply this to your life
Start each day with affirmations; this is how you build a success-driven mindset! It's a way of thinking! A way of being! It's a mindset of success.

Raise Your Standards
You must raise your standards for your life to take off in a different direction. This is critical to your success. It begins by understanding that you are not average, and you should not accept average results. If you have mediocre standards, then you will get mediocre results. You have to be willing to do what others are unwilling to do if you want a better lifestyle. You must also be willing to pay the price for success – which is typically raised standards. Understand that everyone can't go where you're going.

Follow the three action steps below and you'll be well on your way!
1. Create a daily ritual.
2. Practice OQP- Surround yourself with Only Quality People.

3. Take action on your goals and dreams, not tomorrow but TODAY.

Step Into Your Destiny

It's not always easy to design your life. Sometimes you need help figuring out what you want, and sometimes you need help making your dreams a reality. That's where coaching comes in. Coaching can help you create the life you've always wanted. There are many benefits of coaching. Coaching can help you clarify your goals, create a plan and help to achieve them. It can also help you manage stress, improve your communication skills, and boost your self-confidence. What if you could design the life you've always wanted? What would that look like? How would it feel?

If you are ready to Unleash Your Destiny and design the life you love, go to Kelishaworrell.com to sign up for a complimentary coaching consultation. I know you have a dream and vision for your life. So why is it not flourishing? Destiny United Institute has an interactive coaching program that teaches you how to identify the things that hold you back from reaching your full potential. The program gives you the tools that will enable you to achieve your goals, open doors for opportunity, and live a life of purpose. Also, follow me on social media FB or IG @Kelisha Worrell for your daily dose of inspiration.

About Kelisha Worrell

Kelisha Worrell is a #1 International Bestselling Author, Television Host of Destiny Unleashed, Professional Speaker, and Results Coach. She has topped the charts by landing on the front cover of Woman of Dignity Magazine. She has been personally mentored by Bob proctor and given the honor of receiving her speaker's certification by none other than the world's most renowned motivational speaker, Les Brown. Through her coaching, Ms. Worrell equips women with the support, tools, and resources to become successful entrepreneurs, creating an amazing life while having ONE mission, to help you COME BACK STRONGER and share your talents with the world.

Catching Hell on Another Level Became My Blessing

By Dr. Jacquelyn Hadnot

Seldom do we think of going through adversity as a blessing. We consider trials and tribulations as anything other than the universe conspiring against us. We try to avoid the pains and agony that come with adversity. The trials we must endure seem endless with no help in sight. We can decide if we are going to go through the storm or get swept away by the storm.

The trials seem to go without consolation or resolution, and if we are not careful, we will find ourselves murmuring and complaining about the storm. We allow the trials to surround us and rob us of our peace and joy and further sinking us deeper into the muck and mire of despair. The Apostle Paul gave us a clear picture of the troubles we face daily in Second Corinthians 4:8, *We are troubled on every side*... He went on to say, *we are perplexed... Persecuted... cast down...* Paul gave us insight into the attacks we will face as we live our lives for Christ. We are troubled (*afflicted*) on every side, yet not distressed (*crushed*); we are perplexed, but not in despair; Persecuted, but not forsaken (*abandoned*); cast down, but not destroyed (Second Corinthians 4:8-9).

Several years ago, I was diagnosed with Cysts near my brain and tumors in my breast. The doctor informed me that two surgeries were required to avoid Cancer in the future. The growths were growing at an alarming rate, and there was no time to waste. The diagnosis was devastating, and I felt like giving up. This was the moment I knew I was catching hell on another level. I could not wrap my mind around a diagnosis so severe that it would have me contemplating Suicide, but it did, and it was more than I could bear on my own. I needed strength, and I needed a strength and power that NO man could give me. I needed the strength of Jesus.

When we are faced with the most horrendous situation imaginable and think all hope is lost, that is the moment when Jesus must step in and lead and guide us; otherwise, the next step we take might be our last. Nothing makes sense when you are catching hell on another level, and no one can tell you differently. Your faith is now on trial, and you must walk out victorious. 1 Peter 1:6-7 tells us, *Wherein ye greatly rejoice, though now for a season, if need be, ye are in heaviness through manifold temptations: That the trial of your faith, being much more precious than of gold that perisheth, though it be tried with fire, might be found unto praise and honour and glory at the appearing of Jesus Christ* (KJV). You would ask to whom is my trial precious? It is precious to God because He will receive the glory after you have suffered a little while and come through the furnace of affliction without smelling like smoke.

We all go through for a season, and we experience heaviness in untold measures, but regardless of the great measure of tests and trials, our ability to stand and withstand means everything to Our God. Remember, the trial of our faith is more precious than gold. All the gold in the world cannot compare to the honor and glory the Lord receives when we go through, overcome, and give Him the glory for bringing us through. The very thing that we thought was there to destroy us was, in reality, there to purify us of the fragments and debris on the things that have held us in bondage.

When we are going through our season of despair, discouragement, sickness, or marital problems, it might seem as if the walls are crashing around us. Trouble on every side seems like an understatement when the enemy is on every side, and there appears to be no way out. When trouble is on every side, the days seem endless and the nights seem hopeless, and the time in between is immeasurable. This is the day you realize you are catching hell on another level.

The Bible comforts us with these words in Psalm 30:5 ...*weeping may endure for a night, but joy cometh in the morning.* No one knows how long the night will last, and no one can tell when the morning will come, but rest assured, the morning will come. When it arrives, it will bring the light of victory to your life, and it will show God's glory shining brightly because you stood the test and endured like a soldier for the Lord.

You might ask questions such as:
- *Why did I have to suffer?*
- *Why did I have to go through?*
- *Did I do something wrong to bring this devastation to my life?*
- *Is God punishing me for something I did wrong?*
- *What sin did I commit to bring a famine to my life?*

These are a few of the burning questions that go through our finite minds as we try to *"figure out"* why hell is busting us upside the head?

Is catching hell trying to break me, shake me or make me?

I have asked this question a million times, and I have concluded that it is not there to destroy me; it is there to purify me. When I am going through the valley of…, it shakes me out of a comfort zone, shakes me out of complacency, and break off moments of lethargy concerning the things of God.

It is also designed to perfect the things that concern us and bring us to a place of humility, peace, patience, joy, self-control, and more. *But the God of all grace, who hath called us unto his eternal glory by Christ Jesus, after that ye have suffered a while, make you perfect, stablish, strengthen, settle you* (1 Peter 5:10). After going through a period of "suffering," Our awesome God:

- **Perfects** (improves, refines, or sharpens)
- **Establishes** (launches, inaugurates, confirms)
- **Strengthens** (reinforces, fortifies, increases, builds up)

- **Settles** (become peaceful, calm, reconciles) Also (inhabits)

Suffering produces fruit. It might not seem like it when you are going through the fire or the flood, but it will produce fruit as long as we remain in Him. When the fire ignites fruit in us, it begins to activate the spirit fruit juices, and we flow in unprecedented ways. It is an awesome thing to behold when the Lord releases that which is within us as He flows through us, and we flow in Him. We are told in John 15:16, *"Ye have not chosen me, but I have chosen you, and ordained you, that ye should go and bring forth fruit, and that your fruit should remain: that whatsoever ye shall ask of the Father in my name, he may give it you"* (KJV).

What are some of the fruits produced?
The fruit of:
- Peace
- Joy
- Patience
- Faith
- Love
- Trust
- Resilience
- Perseverance
- Obedience
- Self-control

The Furnace of Affliction Will Ignite a Fire In You!

The fires of the furnace of affliction will ignite a fire in you that cannot be explained nor contained. We are told in Isaiah 48:10 that we were chosen in the furnace of affliction. *Behold, I have refined thee, but not with silver; I have chosen thee in the furnace of affliction (Isaiah 48:10 KJV).* What does it mean to be chosen in the furnace of affliction? First, it means that God did not use the cute and cuddly times to process us. God uses our trials and uncomfortable experiences to refine us and purify our hearts.

It is through the uncomfortable times that God has our full attention. We pay close attention to every detail because we are afraid to miss God. Missing Him might mean a delay in coming through the furnace of catching hell. Miss Him might also mean a delay on the road to purpose and destiny.

What does it take to go through the fire or the flood? It takes:

- **Prayer**: Pray without ceasing. (1 Thessalonians 5:17)
- **Repentance**: And saying, Repent ye: for the kingdom of heaven is at hand. (Matthew 3:2)
- **Time alone with God**: Draw nigh to God, and he will draw nigh to you (James 4:8)
- **Obedience**: Submit yourselves, therefore, to God. Resist the devil, and he will flee from you (James 4:7)
- **Clarity**: And the Lord answered me, and said, Write the vision, and make it plain upon tables, that he may run that readeth it (Habakkuk 2:2)
- **Perseverance**: Praying always with all prayer and supplication in the Spirit, and watching

thereunto with all perseverance and supplication for all saints (Ephesians 6:18)
- **Patience**: But in all things approving ourselves as the ministers of God, in much patience, in afflictions, in necessities, in distresses (2 Corinthians 6:4)
- **Faith**: Now faith is the substance of things hoped for, the evidence of things not seen (Hebrews 11:1)

It takes these elements and more because destiny awaits us if we trust in the Lord and follow His directions. You cannot follow the directions if you cannot hear Him; therefore, we must listen to and for the voice of the Lord our God. *So, then faith cometh by hearing, and hearing by the word of God* (Romans 10:17).

The Fire Within

After we have suffered a while, after we have gone through the furnace of affliction, after the floods of adversity have been swept away, God will establish us. *But the God of all grace, who hath called us unto his eternal glory by Christ Jesus, after that ye have suffered a while, make you perfect, stablish, strengthen, settle you* (1 Peter 5:10). The fire and the flood will put you in a place to hear God clearly. As the fire burns within you, it will burn away the fragments and debris of your past. The flood will wash away the residue of Egypt that has hindered you for too long.

As the fire burns within, it will ignite a fire for more of His presence, more of His power, more of His love – it will ignite a fire for MORE! It's in the MORE that you will be like Moses standing on holy ground, watching and waiting for the glory of the Lord to manifest. The Lord will call out to you, saying, *"Seek MY Face!"* Your heart and everything in you will cry with a resounding voice, *"Your face Lord, I will seek."*

Then *Moses* said, *"Please, show me Your glory!"* Jacquie said, *"Please, show me Your glory!"* Allow your heart to cry, *"Please, show me Your glory!"* As the fire burns within you, allow it to set your heart ablaze with more of the presence of the Lord and let your heart cry, *"Please, show me Your glory!"* It's time for the glory of the Lord to arise within us and among us.

There will be days you will face adversity, but let this be the last day that you catch hell on another level and you don't know how to stand and command. This is the last day that you don't have warfare strategies that enable you to defeat the tactics of the enemy. Ask the Lord to train your hands for war and your fingers for battle. Having done all, stand. Stand and watch God destroy the enemy that is raging against you and bring victory to your life and glory to His Holy name. Be blessed.

DR. JACQUIE HADNOT

About Dr. Jacquie Hadnot

Genuine leadership is found amongst those audacious enough to signal the importance of others, to the rest of the world. Trailblazing a path where philanthropy meets world class ingenuity; is the compassionate professional; Dr. Jacquie Hadnot.

Dr. Jacquie Hadnot is an 8x international best-selling author, cleric, entrepreneurial enthusiast, and CEO and

Founder of both, **Mallie Boushaye Essentials** and **Purpose Life Coaching, LLC**. No stranger to establishing anomalous conglomerates, Dr. Hadnot has enjoyed the *flex* of sustaining a six-figure manufacturing and retail business, without compromising the mandate of her life's core intendment; the will to inspire, empower, and implore, people. Reputed for her uncanny ability to shift perspectives, enthuse purpose, and invoke change in diverse clientele, Dr. Jacquie Hadnot remains a highly sought after proponent in the world of business, ministry, and social purlieus.

Her mantra is simple: Dr. Jacquie is led by a conclusive resolve to help individuals attain the strategies they need to succeed in life, because therein lies assured greatness, and that greatness lives in all of humanity.

Dr. Jacquie Hadnot combines unyielding excellence with a sincere regard for education, achievement, and community involvement. She holds a PhD in Pastoral Theology, a MA in Leadership and Education, a BA in Theology, and a degree in Accounting and Business Finance. In accommodation to her propensity for educational acumen, Dr. Jacquie has also attained certifications in life, business, and cancer care coaching. Her contributions in vocation, workshop facilitation, and ministerial advancements are awe-inspiring; as she has not only managed to lead in sales and ethics, but also in creating quintessential forms of humanitarianism, including support groups and multi-dimensional outreach programs. Dr. Jacquie's serviceability has proven highly prolific, as she was the **2022 recipient of the Joe Biden Presidential Lifetime Achievement Award**; easily yielding her one of the most effective leaders of our time.

Whether she is coaching the masses, empowering entrepreneurs, or overseeing her own television network, Dr. Jacquie Hadnot displays no corroboration in slowing down. When she is not out leaving a lasting impression on the world, she is an asset to her local communal body, and a loving member of her family and friendship circles.

Dr. Jacquie Hadnot. Leader. Organizer. Philanthropist.

Identity Crisis
By Dr. Darline Nabbie

When I looked up the definition of identity, I had several questions. The question that continues to resurface is, "Who am I?" Identity is defined as being who or what a person or thing is. After reading how identity is defined, I quickly realized that I had an identity crisis. How does one know who they are?

When I was about six years old, the elementary school I attended held a graduation for all kindergartners. I received three achievement medallions and several certificates. My parents were so proud; they celebrated that moment for months. In my parent's living room, my picture hangs proudly on the wall of me, holding my certificates and wearing my medallions. I had on a cream dress, white stockings, and white shoes in that photo. Looking back to that moment in my life, I realized it was the first time I attached to an identity. Praise felt so good! Seeing the excitement on my parent's faces as I received each certificate has remained ingrained in my mind. I realized as the years went on that moment was difficult to duplicate. I realized that moments are meant to be celebrated. Instead, I became someone who sought out validation. I know now that I spent so many years trying to get back to that moment in time.

When I was about ten years old, my father lost his eyesight to glaucoma. I firmly believe my parents made a vow to each other. I believe that vow was not to let this uncontrollable event rule their marriage and our family. My dad did the best he could to get his vision back. He had a total of over 15 surgeries. I remember realizing that he would not accept complete defeat but instead trust in a power greater than him for his healing. In the meantime, he took on stay-at-home daddy duties seriously, never skipping a beat. As the months went by, the reality began to sink in. I was a girl who had a dad that couldn't see. I didn't understand why us. I figured it was just the way things were meant to be. Bad things happen to me. This uncontrollable event also became my identity.

I played basketball for the first time in 9th grade. I fell in love instantly with the sport of basketball. I poured all of my emotions, all of my passion, and all of my strength into basketball. In one game, my coach said, "Darline, if you keep this up, you will get an athletic scholarship."

I didn't understand what that meant. After he noticed the confusion on my face, he said, "If a college sees your potential the way that I do, they will offer you money to go to college, and you get to play basketball."

It was my parent's dream to go to college, and I loved basketball, so I set a goal to show up to every game playing my best. A couple of coaches saw my potential, just like my high school coach mentioned. I was given a scholarship to play basketball at a division 1 school. I was the first in my family to receive an athletic scholarship. I was amazed at the opportunity to be selected to do something I loved daily and go to college. Division one collegiate basketball was creme de la creme. The Wolfpack community knew how to show up for the teams and cheer us on in a way I had never experienced before. I then went on to play basketball semi-professionally in Germany. I couldn't help but sense disappointment from my parents. I didn't understand why they didn't see this as something great. So, I gave up the game I loved because it wasn't pleasing to others. I didn't know it then, but later on in life, I realized people-pleasing became my identity as I began to read self-development books.

  In my late twenties, I had all these identities. Identities that would dictate how I showed up in every room I walked in. Identities that would cause me to question if living was even worth it. What I learned about identities as I began to really ask God questions was this; I took on those identities and made them my own. That was a choice! The thing about options is you can choose differently. As simple as that is, I learned once you have attached yourself to something and you have settled into that thing, it's hard to let it go.

  For example, I love Apple products. Each time Apple creates something new, I find a reason to need that thing. One year, someone was convinced that Android is just as good as Apple. So, I decided to buy a Samsung Note and try it. In about a month, I brought it back and requested an iPhone. When the sales representative asked me why I wanted to return it, I told him that I had gotten so used to having an iPhone that this Android system was just foreign. I realized that is what detaching from an identity feels like. It felt like second nature to be a people-pleaser. It felt like second nature to walk into a room trying to prove my worthiness. Breaking up with these identities can feel like betrayal. Breaking up with who you thought you were is painful. Although it feels like betrayal and can be painful, it is necessary! If you want to live God's identity for you, you must let all those other identities go.

So back to my original question, how does one know who they are? After asking that question several times over and over, God said, "Have you asked me who you are?"

Struggling with the idea that God could help me figure out my identity, I continued to tackle this alone. Once I felt depleted and wanted to give up, God said, "All those identities you have taken on are all lies. None of those identities define who you truly are. I know who you are and who you are is far greater than what you believe."

So, once I understood that I knew that the identities that I latched onto could be unlatched. I also realized that God would be right beside me as I struggled to let some of those identities go. Some of you might have the same question I had when I realized those identities were lies. How do I begin to let these identities go? The first step is to write all those identities down and burn them. Literally! Some months, I have had to do this several times to remind myself that I am no longer a people-pleaser. I had to remind myself that I was already worthy. For some, it may take one month. For others, it may take six months. For some, it may take longer.

The second step is to write down who God says you are. Even if you don't believe what you are writing when you begin to take on a new identity, it doesn't make it untrue. Everything God starts to tell you about who you are is true! The third step is to surround yourself with people who believe what God says about them. You will have to let go of those individuals who believe what they think about you. Especially if what those individuals believe contradicts what God believes about you. Once you begin to follow these steps, God's voice will get louder and louder until it drowns out all the other voices. You will no longer have an identity crisis but an identity shift. Jeremiah 1:5 says *Before I formed you in the womb, I knew you. Before you were born, I set you apart.* I realized God knew who I was all along. He set me a part of a purpose, so taking on God's identity was crucial to fulfilling God's purpose for me. God knows who you are, and he is patiently waiting on you to join him on your journey.

About Darline Nabbie

Dr. Darline Nabbie is a Military Spouse, Healthcare Executive, Professor, Public Speaker, and Author. Dr. Nabbie was raised in Miami, Florida. She received a full scholarship to play basketball at North Carolina State University, where she received her Bachelor's Degree in Sociology. After graduating, she went to Germany, where she played semi-professional basketball for the

Hallé Lions, where she led the team to the championship game and received a gold medal.

She then returned to the United States and began her healthcare career for the United States Medical Command in 2014. She earned her Master's Degree in Healthcare Administration from Ashford University in 2016 and then earned her Doctorate in Healthcare Administration from Walden University in 2022. She is currently a Healthcare Executive for the United States Medical Command. Dr. Darline Nabbie has over 8+ years of healthcare administrative, operations management, and strategic planning experience. She is also a professor for Georgia Southwestern State University, where she teaches Cross-Cultural Issues for Caregivers. She aspires to become the first woman in her family to hold a C-suite position in healthcare.

This year, Dr. Nabbie has also begun her career as a public speaker advocating for Diversity, Equity, and Inclusion and uplifting the military spouse and veteran community. She is the CEO of Dr. Nabbie Consulting Services. Dr. Nabbie is the first person in her family to earn a doctorate in Healthcare Administration and the first person in her family to become an author.

Email: darline@drnabbieconsultingservices.com
Tic-Tok, Twitter & Instagram: DrD_Speaks

Born Leader, Designed By God
By Tara Nicole Green

When a child is conceived and matures in its mother's womb, it will develop personality and characteristics. Leadership is one of those virtues. Refined as early as infant age, the capability to lead by example while strategizing a successful plan ultimately meets the goal at hand. Leadership qualities can be learned. However, natural-born leaders instinctively can initiate the leadership quality required for any situation. Usually, there is no challenge or long gap in time for a clear resolution to come to the leader. Nonetheless, this ability is unlearned, and the individual does not control it.

According to Dictionary.com (2022), the word lead is the act of going before and showing or guiding. The definition also implies that one model and guides and there are followers. Furthermore, an individual is at a level to the extent of such an advanced position. This means that the leader holds the rank or status of one who is advanced in a specific position. They are far beyond or advanced to those they lead.

A Born Leader cannot turn on and off a switch of leading; this is part of their being and is who they are. The leader's actions or character will show up in all aspects of their lives. As we see it demonstrated in the word of God, Elijah was a leader, and Elisha was the student. This means that any leader must have some training or guidance to build the necessary skills, characteristics, or even endurance to fulfill the role as the leader and the purpose, assignment, or need that should be fulfilled.

Leading sometimes will come with costs. When one takes the lead, they are in the position where everything demonstrated, conscious and unconscious, is being watched or seen by those observing. Usually, those viewing from the outside do not understand the mountainous and strenuous encounters of stretching, conflict, and strife that may come with leading.

Born Leaders are unstoppable and demonstrate endurance. They continue to press no matter what the circumstance. When leaders collide with challenges that cause significant stress and pain, they will bear all that comes with any circumstance. This does not mean that it does not hurt or that they are not impacted. It only means that they embrace it all until there is relief and the affliction has ceased. While enduring calamity, leaders will always maintain an attitude of serving. No matter what amount of weight they carry, a leader will always find the strength to meet the need of others as well as put others first.

As referenced in Matthew 14:1-31, the story demonstrates true servanthood when Jesus went to a deserted place to be by himself and grieve over his cousin John's execution. However, the multitude followed Jesus on foot from their cities to go where Jesus was. They found him and Jesus unselfishly diverted focus away from his own need to mourn by himself and focus on the needs of the masses needs. Jesus responded to the great multitude not by telling them to go away so that he could grieve in sadness, but he had compassion and healed the sick and fed them all. A leader's servant attitude is only demonstrated because they rely on God's strength and not their own. Such as we see in Matthew, the example of Jesus.

Operating a significant level of faith and taking risks are characteristics that leaders naturally possess. God's plan for leaders may not always be mapped out in detail. There is a level of trust that a leader must have in God to know that each path is leading them to their destiny or purpose in life. The leader must understand that everything will work out, although they do not see what the end will look like or know the final outcome.

We are reminded in Hebrews 11:1, "Now faith is the substance of things hoped for, the evidence of things not seen." A true Born Leader must lean on the word and have faith in the word. Another scripture that reigns true to this statement is James 2:14-26 (NLV) "What good is it, dear brothers and sisters if you say you have faith but don't show it by your actions? Can that kind of faith save anyone?" The leader must know that their actions will testify to their level of faith.

Discernment abides within Born Leaders. The ability to lean on the direction of God for every situation and allow God's guidance to determine their actions. The leader does not take control but only counts on the prompting of the Holy Spirit by casting down the flesh and leaning on God. It is referenced in Proverbs 3:6-7 (NLT), "Seek his will in all you do, and he will show you which path to take. Don't be impressed with your own wisdom. Instead, fear the Lord and turn away from evil." The referenced text identifies the ability of the leader to choose. However, a Born Leader does not take their own will but that of our heavenly father. According to Romans 12:1 (NLT), "And so, dear brothers and sisters,[a] I plead with you to give your bodies to God because of all he has done for you. Let them be a living and holy sacrifice—the kind he will find acceptable. This is truly the way to worship him." God honors our willingness to surrender and returns blessings for our obedience.

    Leaders exhibit qualities of love and illustrate the open hand of giving. The word of God states in 2 Corinthians 6:6-8, "Remember this: Whoever sows sparingly will also reap sparingly, and whoever sows generously will also reap generously. 7 Each of you should give what you have decided in your heart to give, not reluctantly or under compulsion, for God loves a cheerful giver. 8 And God is able to bless you abundantly, so that in all things at all times, having all that you need, you will abound in every good work."

    The word of God further speaks to qualities of love and giving together in 2 Corinthians 8:7 (NIV) *"But since you excel in everything—in faith, in speech, in knowledge, in complete earnestness, and in the love we have kindled in you[a]—see that you also excel in this grace of giving. 8 I am not commanding you, but I want to test the sincerity of your love by comparing it with the earnestness of others. 9 For you know the grace of our Lord Jesus Christ, that though he was rich, yet for your sake, he became poor, so that you through his poverty might become rich."*

Operating in the fruit of the gifts also resides within the born leader. According to Galatians 5:22-23 (NIV), *"But the fruit of the Spirit is love, joy, peace, forbearance, kindness, goodness, faithfulness, gentleness, and self-control. Against such things there is no law."* These attributes are innate and nest within the leader. The fruits of the spirit transpire as naturally as breathing.

When a Born Leader utilizes all gifts, talents, and skills, there is no question that they are equipped with all that is needed to execute any assignment or task set before them. Essentially, this is what a leader is designed for. Understanding their gifts and embracing them all empowers the Born Leader to ignite the flame inside and run with the power. All who come into contact are empowered, fulfilled, and revived. Be encouraged to acknowledge your unique gifts and talents. Let the flame in you light up the world.

References

© 2022 Dictionary.com, LLC
New International Version (NIV)
Holy Bible, New International Version®, NIV® Copyright ©1973, 1978, 1984, 2011 by Biblica, Inc.® Used by permission. All rights reserved worldwide.
NIV Reverse Interlinear Bible: English to Hebrew and English to Greek. Copyright © 2019 by Zondervan.

About Tara N. Green

- Business professional with over 20 years of business management experience in Fortune 500 companies. Areas of knowledge- Finance and Accounting, Commercial Leasing Accounting/Finance, and Risk.

- Adjunct Professor – Teach course subjects in Business, Professional Development, and Accounting/Finance.
- B.S. in Business Administration, Accounting from DeVry University, and dual master's degrees in Business Administration, Accounting, as well as a master's in Project Management from Keller University. Currently, pursuing a Doctorate in Business.
- Dedication to inspiring others and making her community a better place by conducting empowerment workshops for young girls aged 6 to 18 years old, on topics such as money, savings, budgeting, and goal setting.
- Believer in the power of volunteerism and service. While serving as Chair from 2016-2019, raised over 46K for United Negro College Fund recipients.
- Enjoys cooking, gardening, and watching movies with her husband.
- Humble Servant and Worshiper of God. Faithful believer of the word of God.
- Prayer Warrior and Intercessor

Contact Tara:
https://www.facebook.com/TaraGreenthepinnaclestrategist

Re-Ignited to Walk in Power
By Laila Miller

---

*I*GNITED to SERVE. What do you think of when you say that out loud? It makes me think of someone EXCITED to do something for someone else or for a cause!

The word Ignite means- to catch fire or cause to catch fire. But what is it that causes the actual igniting for you? There must be something that sparks the flame.

I believe that spark would be *passion*. It all starts with PASSION. Passion is the fire that ignites us to act! Passion is a driving force. It inspires us. It pushes us forward. It gives us something to look forward to. It gives us hope. Without it, we would remain stagnant.

So, the question now is, what is your passion? Look back at your life. What were the moments you have found yourself stirred up enough to want to take action? Something that excited you.

For me, SERVING is what ignites me!! But before I go into that. Let me share what took place for me to get back on track to "serving" God's way.

HOW I got Re-Ignited: A Story of REDEMPTION

When you're in the middle of the storm and facing your darkest hours, sometimes you think, "This is it. It's the end. How will God ever be able to turn my life around?"

I had a chapter, a season in my life just like that. Moments of staring out my window, watching neighbors in their homes wondering what their lives were like? Were they happy? Were they struggling like me? I spent countless moments planning how I could save myself, break out of the box, break out of the depression that made me see only DARKNESS. It was horrible. I was a minister's daughter. I was a minister myself, and I was married to a minister. I was supposed to be perfect!! But I wasn't. I had hit a wall, was broken, and falling apart!

It's wild how life can throw so many twists and turns. It's AMAZING how GOD sees the end of that season – the end of that chapter and knows just how to redeem your life!!

Fast forward years later – just the other day, I found myself driving up to the house that brought me so much pain. Where my marriage was falling apart. Where I was burning out on Ministry. Where I hit rock bottom and could only see the dark.

YES! I drove up, looked at that house, and said out loud, "LOOK AT ME NOW."

I am sitting outside this house, and I am a NEW person! HAPPY, completed, loved, believed in, BLESSED on all levels of life! At that time, the ironic thing was that I lived in Minnesota for two years. My marriage finally fell apart, and I went back home to New Jersey. NOW, here I am again! In the same town years later, living a completely DIFFERENT life! HOW did it come full circle? HOW would I end up back here!?! GOD'S PLAN. And here I am. ONLY GOD... HE saw, HE knew all along!

    This is only a part of my story. But, driving up to that house the other day was wild, to say the least. It makes me emotional when I think of HOW MUCH God loves me, saw me, stood by me, and REDEEMED me!! I. AM. SO. THANKFUL. And, I have been RE-ignited to serve once again!

    Being a woman of power can mean so many different things to different people. For me, power comes from the presence of God. A powerful Woman knows who she is in Christ. She understands the authority of being a believer. She knows God. And she knows how to hear His voice so she can take action in fulfilling what He has planned for her that specific day. Serving is always part of the plan somehow because God's heart is for people.

    Servanthood is spoken about throughout the Bible. The very theme is all about serving others. Look at the life of Jesus. He served continually. He served all people. People of different ethnicities. People who believed differently. People from all social classes. A true servant brings healing, is a listener, and brings growth and awareness to others. A faithful servant loves the loveless and is a safe place for the lonely and brokenhearted. I can say I am the best version of myself when serving others!

Servanthood is a gift. We are all given gifts to work with. There are different capacities of serving. We are not going to be good at them all. We can try. But the ones we are "gifted" in, we will thrive in! How does God use you to connect to others? What comes easy for me may not be easy for you. But that does not mean you are not gifted to serve. You have a niche. You just need to find it. Ask yourself, how does God use you to connect to others? In finding the answer to this question, you will find your niche. It may be volunteering at church, visiting the elderly, being a part of a charity, or starting YOUR OWN charity! The list goes on and on. We are ALL gifted to serve in some capacity. How do I know this? Because we were made in HIS image. Jesus was a servant. He served every day of his life. Therefore, we are made to serve!

Here is what many of my days look like when serving. I like to call them "God Encounters."

It started when I was a young girl. I was 20 years old, and my husband and I started a church. Since the church was young, my husband worked during the day. I was pregnant with our son, Pauly, and stayed home. The call of God was strong, and I was determined to serve- to allow God to use me in changing lives. I started by going to a hospital in Newark, NJ.

At that time, many of the floors were designated for HIV patients, along with Tuberculosis. I would go to the hospital and pray with these people. Many times, families were in the room and they were emotional as to what was taking place with their loved ones. Boldy, I would walk in, introduce myself, and share God's love. I saw what HIV and Tuberculosis could do to a person. I saw the pain and could smell death. BUT I was not moved. I was God inside minded! I knew who I was and the power there was in the Name of Jesus! These were glorious days. I watched as God moved with salvations and healings! Fast forward to today, and I can tell you other stories of walking in power, ignited to serve the Kingdom of God! For me, this is what life is all about, SERVING people, sharing a word to encourage, extending God's love, and allowing God to move through you wherever you are each day!

For whoever is reading this, I pray you will allow God to take you places you've never gone before in serving, walking in the power of God, and watching Him move through you!

About Laila Miller

Laila Miller is a mother and wife first. Family is everything.

    Laila began full-time ministry as a young girl of 19 years of age. Serving early on as Associate Pastor, from there, she pioneered her own church, and later transitioned to traveling as a speaker both nationally & internationally. Laila is also gifted as an entrepreneur and runs two successful businesses alongside her husband, Jeff.

She has earned two degrees and is an Ordained Minister and Licensed Life Coach. She is a motivator and has a genuine heart and love for all people. Outside of the church, she also speaks motivationally to Women in the Pageant world, Business World, and other similar groups.

Laila is actively involved with a sister Duo-Sorella LIVE, which is a podcast & social media outreach. She and her sister Elisa speak to and motivate women all over the world!
In her free time, Laila and her husband Jeff enjoy traveling and surrounding themselves with their beautiful family.

Sorella LIVE @ Facebook
sorella.live @ IG
Website: https://sorellaministries.live/

I Am The One
By Shaquatta Edgar

I worked as a certified nursing assistant for seven years. I made beds, cleaned bottoms, gave baths, cooked, cleaned, completed errands, checked vital signs, etc. That was my job. It took a lot of patience to deal with the many different personalities and attitudes of my clients. So many times, I wanted to walk off the job and quit. No matter how many times a client cussed me out or fussed at me, I kept on serving. Most were elderly, and I had to consider every client as a family member. They needed me whether they wanted me in their home or not. Most of the time, they would come back around and apologize for treating me badly.

I never said as a child that when I grow up, I want to be a Certified Nursing Assistant. Neither did I say I wanted to be a minister. However, we don't get to choose what we are called to do. I am glad I got to experience the humility of being a Certified Nursing Assistant. Serving others takes a lot of humility and patience. That doesn't mean people are supposed to walk all over you and mistreat you. Neither should we allow them to. I feel like being a Certified Nursing Assistant was one of the things that prepared me for the call of a minister. Not everyone can do certain lowly positions, not because of ability but because some people have nasty attitudes and will misuse people for their gain.

Most of my life was spent hiding, being quiet, and allowing others to surpass me. Today, there has been a major shift. So, no more hiding, no more being quiet, and no more mediocrity. I am a light, and I was born to shine. I have been called to the frontlines by challenges in my life. At first, I allowed my challenges to keep me from progressing. I was in a place called stuck. My life was not meant to be stuck but to be an example of greatness.

For something to be great, it has to go through a process of molding. I would say my molding began at a young age. Trips back and forth to the doctor with my mom to see an orthopedic specialist. I was the little girl people saw tripping up over her own feet because her feet were turned inward. I remember wearing corrective shoes to bed and being in pain. As I got a little older, the cartilage in my knee began to wear out. My knee would become inflamed and swell and do all kinds of popping. At times the pain was unbearable. By the age of fourteen, I was undergoing my first knee surgery. Then a year later, I was getting my second knee surgery to replace cartilage in my knee. Growing up with juvenile arthritis was very challenging. There were things I wanted to do but couldn't. I remember signing up for basketball in high school, but I couldn't try out because I had to get knee surgery. I had to be administered my SATs at home because I was still recovering from knee surgery. Going through that didn't stop me from graduating high school with an overall A average and 4.0 GPA.

At the age of fourteen, I had also given my life to Christ. Sometimes I used to instruct the young kids at church during Sunday school, not knowing that I was called to inspire youth and be a servant for God like I am today. It blows my mind how God led me through all these years on a journey that, at times, I often took for granted. I see now so clearly that I am the one. I am the one that had to go through in order to get to. We are so quick to focus on the happy ending that we don't even take the time to close our eyes and realize how truly blessed we are in the midst of where we are. My God, if we could only just stop and take a look at where we are right now. Where we are at this very moment in our lives has a purpose. Someone didn't make it to this moment, but we did. That means we have another opportunity to make an impact in the world.

When I began to take my focus off all the things that were going on in my life and focus on my purpose, I became more productive. Our lives don't have to be perfect to have meaning. So what I'm a single mother, So what I've been divorced. That doesn't stop me or define who I am! I still have a purpose. I am the first teacher that my daughter learns from. That lets me know that I can't be listening to or watching anything around her. I can't act any kind of way and dress any kind of way either. My serving starts at home before it goes anywhere else. I may slow down for a break, but I will not quit. I will stay on the course that has been set before me to follow.

All the challenges in my life have ignited me and given me a brand-new look at my calling. It made me realize that I am the one that has to stand up and stand out. Everyone isn't going to like how God is raising me up. I can't worry about that or take offense. They weren't there with me through my storms, but God was and still is. Several years ago, I allowed what someone said to hold me back from serving the people. I know now that I don't need approval or validation from man to do what God has led me to do. God was preparing me for the ministry He placed on the inside of me. Everything we do for God is not inside the four walls of a building. I am the one that takes God everywhere I go. Also, some relationships in our lives are only for a season and to serve a specific purpose. That is why we can't take everyone along with us. Some people we have to surpass in order to be the blessing we need to be in the Earth.

We can also miss out on what God wants to bless us with because we decided to stay behind and accept whatever comes our way. God gave His son so I could have an abundant life, not a sad, miserable life. You can have all the fun and pleasures in this life, but your life will not have fulfillment if you are not walking in purpose. We will just be bouncing from place to place without making an impact. I am moving past all the distractions and staying in purpose in this season. That is what matters. Serving isn't glitz and glamor. There will be some tears, sweat, frustration, and even anger. It is exciting to know that what I do is helping someone else. Even Jesus himself said He didn't come to be ministered to but to minister. A lot of people in this life want to be waited on hand and foot instead of serving.

Serving is not giving so you can get in return. Serving is selflessly providing a need to someone else without partiality to their gender, race, ethnicity, age, or belief. I know that what I do for others, I do for God. I can't look over feeding someone that doesn't like me and feed everyone that does. As a servant, I have to sometimes put others' concerns before my own and regard them better than I do myself. My heart posture has to be submissive, so I can be understanding, compassionate and loving towards others.

We can't help the people in the world running from every issue and every problem. However, we can lead them by enduring those not-so-good moments in our lives. There is joy at the end of a breakthrough, and there can also be joy in the process. So, when life happens, I will just keep on going knowing that someone out there is watching and following me. I can't allow my past struggles to keep me from reaching higher to make a difference in this broken world. I used to think not finishing college made me less than all my friends that did finish. I no longer compare myself because we all have our own journey. Whether I have a degree or not, I am worthy. My fulfillment is not in a degree but in my purpose. No degree could prepare me for the things I have experienced in life. Having the courage to go through several storms back-to-back and still be here to encourage others is a blessing that I am grateful for. Serving others does not exempt me from life's hardships, but it allows others to see me as human. I was built in the process of my challenges to be durable and tough. I have been given the strength and the power to overcome it all.

I am the one that God called to intercede on behalf of my family and others. Waking up at 3 am can be challenging, but it is necessary. I would be short changing myself if I didn't get out of my bed to pray. I gain strength and focus when I pray. I am the blessing that was placed here in the Earth to bless somebody else. I didn't get where I am today by having it all together.

Some days were hectic and full of disappointment, and I wanted to escape it all. Some days, I felt unsure of what I was here for. I even asked, Why me? However, today I am sure, and why not me. I wasn't created to run and hide but to be bold as a lion. I constantly speak affirmations over my life. Speaking what isn't, so what can be, become what is. When others come into my presence, they can feel loved and not rejected. They can talk to me and not have their business all over town. They can experience an advocate who won't turn them away but stand up for them. That is why I was chosen to defend, to protect. I know what it is like to feel alone, rejected, unloved, and afraid. No one should feel this way or be bullied into staying quiet. We all deserve to be heard whether we are speaking or not.

It took a pandemic to show some people that a servant is essential. We need more than just ourselves to accomplish things in life. I may not have everything you want, but I can guarantee that you will get what you need. Don't miss out on what God has placed on the inside of me for your good. My ability to attend to the needs of someone else goes far beyond my outward appearance. Look at my heart. My influence in this world will be mighty. As long as I remain in God, He will abide in me, and with God, all things that I set my heart to do is possible. There are no limitations in the kingdom of God; neither is there lack. As I go about doing God's business, I know He will take care of every one of my needs. There is so much to be done, yet I know I am not alone. God has set all things in motion, and His plan for my life is good. I want God to be pleased with me. I will remain humble as God opens doors for me to spread hope to the world. No one else can complete my assignment for me. I must, and I will press on to the finish line and fulfill my purpose because I am the one.

SHAQUATTA EDGAR

About Shaquatta Edgar

Shaquatta Edgar is the mother of one beautiful and smart Queen. Shaquatta was called by God to be a Chosen Defender for the people. She is anointed to lead and intercede. This powerful voice of thunder can be heard on her Chosen Defender podcast on Anchor, Spotify, YouTube, and Google Podcast. This is one voice you don't want to miss. Shaquatta speaks with boldness, confidence, and her God-given authority. She is a flame thrower in the Holy Ghost.

Shaquatta is birthing all that God has placed on the inside of her, and she isn't backing down! She was anointed and appointed for such a time as this. She's walking in her now and reaching out and snatching souls from the grips of hell with the love of God. She started Greater Love Ministries in her home and has led many nightly devotions and prayer. You can follow this Chosen Defender on FaceBook at Greater Love Ministries 18 and Passion4thepeople. She can also be followed on Instagram, Clubhouse, and Twitter.

Her tribulations have prepared her to be the minister she needs to be to reach the world. She is excited about all that God is doing through her and in her life. She keeps fighting no matter what she has been through because she is an overcomer. Shaquatta is an Amazon #1 Best-selling author in the anthology "Called to Intercede: Praying for Children Volume 8" and also a writer for Gifted Magazine and will very soon have multinational best sellers. She is a ghostwriter for her business Write Impact Ghostwriting Services. She believes that her challenges were a setup to pull all the greatness out of her. This global influencer is soaring higher in God to fulfill the works of the Kingdom. Keep up with this Chosen Defender because God is doing a great work in her.

SHAQUATTA EDGAR

Email:
minshaquattaedgar@gmail.com
website:
https://sites.google.com/view/writeimpactghostwritingservice/home

If Not You, Then Who?
By Deidre A. Calcoate

As I sit here at my desk in late April 2022, windows and doors open, birds chirping, wind chimes going, I cannot help but think about my blessings! I am blessed to be chosen to tell my story, support others on their journey, and be happy to continue learning to accept Who and Whose I AM. I am eternally grateful to my Lord and Savior for his favor, mercy, and faith in me. Blessed that the Lord turned my anger and hurt into a drive to heal, lead with my heart, and support others. I look back and feel pleased with myself in the realization that my best was good enough.

Being a servant leader is a journey that I was called to over 35 years ago. I had the honor and pleasure of serving Arizona's children and families in many capacities throughout my years. There were lessons to be learned and greatness to be expressed. Some lessons came easy, while others were really hard; some made me feel like my journey was great, and others dropped me to my knees.

I started as a manager, not a leader, and I did not know the difference. As a daycare director, I decided to terminate a person I supervised over the telephone for not being able to fulfill their job duties. No doubt about it, this was not appropriate and was not the way a leader would have handled the situation. I believed I had provided sufficient training, coaching, and mentorship but allowing them not to be their highest and best was a disservice to the person, the children, and the families we served. I was not afraid of being harmed; I merely did not have the skill to handle it differently. I know I did my best at the time, but that does not negate the fact that my actions were not that of a leader but a manager. I was extremely hard on myself; for years, I prayed for forgiveness and guidance.

As I grew in my understanding of leadership, I realized holding shame was not helpful, and to do better, I had to learn to be better. I was on a mission to be a great servant leader and do my highest and best, but my life's traumas were holding me hostage and would not allow me to be great. You see, I grew up in a home where belittling, chastising and physical punishment were more common than praise and physical affection. I was frequently told and believed that God was not pleased with me, but thanks to God's earth angels, who have supported me, I came to find comfort in being a child of the Most High King and recognizing He loves me dearly.

Over the years, I served children and families through state government and nonprofit organizations. I held positions in case management, where I served children who had high medical needs and investigated allegations of abuse and neglect. I licensed parents who wanted to foster children and became the Bureau Chief responsible for supporting frontline workers, assessing, and leading the practice of how we served children and families involved with the child welfare system, among other positions. I feel honored and blessed that I could embrace such responsibilities as I know there was supernatural healing that had to have taken place within me. I had been physically and verbally abused growing up, and to turn my pain into my passion was not easy; in fact, it was downright hard. My faith sustained me and allowed me to keep moving through my life challenges.

I have learned valuable leadership and life lessons. There were times when my arrogance showed as I just knew I had all the answers. My lessons seemed to come fast and furious, parents took me to task daily, threatened to sue me, and taught me how to "take my shoes off" when I entered their homes and respect their choices when possible.

Supervisors who were micromanagers taught me how <u>not</u> to lead and the art of being a servant leader. I learned from incredibly smart and caring people who cared about the well-being of children and families and who were not afraid to challenge the system's status quo. Even with that being the case, there were sleepless nights when my prayers did not console me. I wondered whether I had made appropriate decisions. Were the children I left in the family home going to be ok? Did I do all I could to preserve the family unit before making a decision of imminent danger? Was I "cut out" for this work? Although I say my prayers did not console me, I really did not want the answer I was receiving "if not you, then who?"

Working in the child welfare system is hard. Seeing individuals at their worst and making decisions about children's health, welfare, and safety can be overwhelming. My past and feelings had to be kept in check. My heart broke for children who were removed from their families due to abuse and neglect, and my heart hurt for the parents who did not have the skill or support to nurture their children safely. I was once told, by the attorney of a teenager, that the youth would never admit to being abused or neglected ever again due to the distress felt from being placed in foster care. Did I make a mistake in this removal? Was there a different outcome that could have been garnered to keep the child safe? Possibly, but I did the best I could with the information provided. Things were not black and white, there seemed to always be gray, and I was taught to err on the side of safety. I had to know that I had done my best, which was all I could do. I was in constant prayer – praying I made good decisions, never did more harm than good and left families with dignity and value.

I left state service to work with the most remarkable family run organization, where I learned it was ok to "lead with my heart," the importance of our language, and how vital it is to listen to children and families. I understood the power of our words to either build someone up or to tear down. Can you see how God was working on me and through me?

One beautiful day I received a telephone call from the state's adoption manager telling me they were leaving the position and encouraging me to apply. I did not believe I had the skill to be the adoption manager; besides, how could I advocate for children to be adopted when my own experience had not been the best. But wait - my daughter was adopted at ten days old, and she was thriving. I was so confused, part of me was excited, and the other was scared. Should I apply? What if they chose me? I was reminded that God qualifies those He calls, and again I heard, "if not you, then who?"

I submitted to His will, accepted the position, and took on the leadership responsibilities for statewide adoptions and foster care licensing. I AM so proud of the work our team accomplished during my tenure. We took responsibility for supporting case managers in finding forever homes and collaborated with the community and other agencies to give our best to the children. I asked each team member to be the champion for an older child, and to this day, I hear about the connection some continue to have with the children, even into adulthood!

I was in the zone, motivating and supporting others by telling my story, speaking about the importance of sibling bonds, talking about the importance of family, and enjoying being of service. Until one day, our division leader asked me to come to their office. All I could think was, what did I do this time, all of the strides we were making, and I still lacked confidence! I was asked to take a temporary assignment leading the child welfare case management portion. My initial response was unequivocally NO - but God said differently. I was reminded of how I frequently talk about being a collaborator, stepping up to the plate, being a servant leader, and so on and so forth! Again, confusion set in, something inside me was beaming with joy and pride that I was chosen, and there was also something inside of me telling me I was not good enough. I was no longer responsible only for my actions; I was in a leadership role to support and encourage front-line staff across the state. I was accountable for the actions of others.

During that time, there were significant shifts and changes to the child welfare system, there were administration changes, and I was invited to continue in my position. This time I knew Whose I was, and I said yes without much hesitation! A couple of weeks prior, I had received a call from my Bishop, a call that I can imagine a father would make to his child. He made it plain and clear that I was not sitting in someone else's seat, that I had been chosen for this time and place, and I needed to be still and know! So, I did; I completed the assignment and moved into other service positions.

During the pandemic, I suffered the loss of friends and family and decided I wanted more out of life. I enrolled in a personal development course, which has changed the trajectory of my life. I was taught the Universe loves speed and what I was seeking was seeking me. So, I jumped, I retired, and have not looked back. I started Go Within Not Without LLC and further developed my transformation life coaching skills; I AM a bestselling author and a Brainspotting Practitioner. I AM showing up and showing out! I AM here for me and you and am grateful for the blessing.

    I invite you to never, never, never give up! Listen to that still small voice inside, follow your dreams, and remember Whose and Who you are. I pray for your strength and God's mercy. If there is support you desire, I AM ready, willing, and capable of supporting you.

Acknowledgments

First and foremost, I give all honor and praise to God. I recognize that to whom much is given, much is required, and I know I fit into that category. I consider myself blessed to have had two sets of parents – one that provided my genes and another who raised me.

Apostle Deborah Allen – thank you, thank you, thank you. Your encouragement, coaching, and support of me have shown I am a writer! Your confidence in me, I have borrowed many times, and I AM grateful there is no return policy. May God continue to bless you.

Dr. Pamela Henkel, you are an amazing woman of God, and I appreciate you so much in my life. Your belief in me has given me the confidence to jump and grow my wings on the way down.

Readers, thank you for being here. I invite you to believe in yourself and follow your wildest dreams. The world is waiting for you to show up and show out! So, write the book, sing the song, dance like everyone is watching, and pursue your heart's desires.

To my ride or die, sounding board, protector, and so much more, Jonnie Dean Lewis, thank you for your unwavering support; I love you, baby! Dominik, Sophiah, and Mia – Gaga loves you.

To the best friends and family a woman could imagine – I love you with my entire heart. You remain in my prayers and thoughts.

About Deidre Ann Calcoate

Being a late discovery adoptee Deidre Ann Calcoate's career and life mimicked each other. Prior to dedicating her time serving others through transformational life coaching at Go Within Not Without, LLC, Deidre served children and families in Arizona through public agencies responsible for child welfare, behavioral health, and developmental disabilities. She is a 2X best-selling author, international motivational speaker, suicide interventionist, and brainspotting practitioner.

Deidre is a Spelman graduate, mother of 1 and grandmother to 3. Deidre is a passionate advocate for children. She is an avid reader and enjoys supporting others on their journey to being their highest and best.

You can find out more about her Coaching and Brainspotting practice at:
Www.gowithinnotwithout.com, Facebook – Deidre.a.calcoate, Instagram – dcalcoate2, LinkedIn - https://www.linkedin.com/in/deidre-calcoate-gowithinnotwithout/

Leaders Lead
By Sonia Merrit

You were called upon to be a servant leader. Who is a servant leader? Someone on a mission, has a purpose, and is ready to help with change. Kindness is one of the superpowers of leaders; the two go hand in hand. Always Value others for what they are offering, no matter if it doesn't align with your beliefs. To be a leader does not mean you are a controller, and it must be done your way; you have to be willing to listen without judgment. Be a caring person to all you come in contact with; you never know what a difference you will make in that person's life. We are all just visitors passing through this planet. Always be ready to trust others. Have humility; don't make it about you. As we lead others, there are ways to help lift up and guide them along the way.

What are some servant leadership skills? Leaders are born that way; a good heart is invaluable as a leader. Start with excellence and credibility. As leaders, we are called upon to serve, love, guide, share, be patient, and inspire others. Leaders are givers and should make it a practice to give on a regular basis. Leaders are kind and generous people willing to give of themselves. Having compassion and a good sense of community are good qualities of a leader. Go out in your community and find out where you can be of service as a volunteer. As leaders, we should be gracious in our service. I have been in situations where an event was chaotic, and no one was in charge; I used the opportunity to get up and be the leader. I would ask who is in charge? If there is no one, I would step up and take over until the lead person comes in. That demonstrates what a leader is supposed to do, be ready to fill in at a moment's notice and serve.

Many servant leaders have been here before and taught us all about being a great leader. Jesus was a great leader; he healed people as he journeyed along and taught his followers to be compassionate and kind to everyone, not just their inner circle.

Martin Luther King Jr was a leader; he gave us the "I have a dream speech" he spoke about justice when he witnessed how his people were treated, and he asked them to assemble peacefully. Men, women, and children all got involved and started following him; he reminded them to be peaceful since he doesn't promote violence.

Mother Teresa, she made a vow to help one poor person at a time since it was impossible to help the masses all at once, so she could continue to help the less fortunate. She trained others to do the same, and today her work is being continued all throughout the world.

Mahatma Ghandi was a positive influence on the people of India. They all love and respect him. This is a famous quote by him "Be the change you wish to see in the world". I live by this quote. These are some of our great leaders of the past who have left countless examples here for us to follow. We must always look for ways to serve, not to be served.

We also have some modern day leaders who are all around us. Oprah Winfrey started a school in Africa and adopted all the children so she could nurture and guide them. Introduce them to a different culture with her guidance. She is considered what we call a servant leader.

As I was growing up, there were many people in my community. I can now look back and consider them servant leaders—Ms. Rawlins taught countless young women the art of sewing. My grandfather was a local preacher in the church and did serve everyone. He would sit in for the minister. Every Sunday at 8 AM, he would walk over to the Methodist church, which was about 15 minutes from our house, and ring the great big bell, which was located strategically where the sound could echo and be heard for a mile or so.

One day he took all the children with him to teach us the techniques of ringing the bell; it was so heavy we never went with him again. He did it with no effort, but for us, it was tough to pull; it had to be done in a rhythmic sound so they could tell the difference from the other church bells in the area. It reminded the neighborhood, surrounding community, and all churchgoers that service would be in an hour. Then he will get back to church to ring it again for the start of service at 9:00 AM.

My grandpa was a man of God who was highly respected in the community as a leader. He was a contractor who built houses all over the island. As a child growing up, I remembered that if someone was building a house and couldn't afford to hire him, they would come by and ask if he could help them. They would bring the plan for the home after studying it; he would estimate what materials were needed so they could purchase and have it on the lot ready. Sunday after church, he would organize the men in the neighborhood to help with the construction. The owner would buy the material to build the house; they would also cook food to feed the workers.

He would go religiously every Sunday until the house was completed. He was a person I consider to be a servant leader. My grandpa always told us it's better to give than receive. If you said you were going to do something, do it. Leaders lead; don't wait for someone else to step up; you do it if it needs to be done, especially in church or helping out in our community. Dr. Myles Monroe reminds us to always walk with God. As we go about our daily lives, there are always opportunities to be servant leaders all around us.

About Sonia Merrit

Sonia is a wedding and event planner who wears many hats. She helps clients to transform their events from great to fabulous. She also uses the lessons she learned to inspire others and help transform the lives of her family, community, and people all over the world. Born and raised on the beautiful island of St.

Kitts, Sonia is helping others find and raise their voices, just as she's learned to do through her writing.

She is the oldest of twelve children, raised by a single mother, and has played many roles in her family. She's seen heartache and joy come together when you would least expect it. She's also seen conflict and resolution when people work out their problems accidentally and intentionally.

Sonia is a confidence and mindset coach who brings the skills she's acquired throughout her life to help you to find clarity and purpose.

She's here to help you work out whatever is bothering you and help you choose which role you'd like to play to stay engaged with your family, no matter how complicated their lives are: mediator, healer, helper, troublemaker, and nurturer. Which role would you like to play?

Sonia is a wife and the mother of three beautiful children.

She's also a Contributing Author of "WOMEN OF THE POWER VOICE," an international bestseller. She graduated from Les Brown's "Power Voice Program" and Jon Talarico's "Thinking Into Results Program."

To contact Sonia
IG Soniasdreamevents
FB Sonia merit
Messenger
Merrit.sonia@gmail.com

+6650

The Power Of Saying Yes
By LaKeisha Richards

"If somebody offers you an amazing opportunity, but you are not sure you can do it, say yes – then learn how to do it later." ~Richard Branson

Welcome and Congratulations to The Power and Season of YES!

I remember as a little girl growing up, I had so many wonderful dreams of what I thought my life would look like as an adult. I dreamt of traveling the world and serving the world by using my voice to sing and minister to people on major platforms with some of the greatest Gospel artists in our nation. Boy, was I in for a big surprise, not to mention never imagining all the U-Turns that I would have to take on this journey called life. However, there's nothing wrong with wishful thinking, right? 😊

Who would have ever known the freedom and strength a person receives when saying YES? It was just two years ago that our nation was faced with a global pandemic that not only did we not see coming, but not everyone was prepared! It wasn't just one specific state, family, ethnicity, or religion that was impacted.

Everyone felt, and many are still feeling, the impact of this global pandemic. However, I must say, as tragic as it was, it has caused everyone to shift in certain areas of their lives—some for the better and some for the worst. Many became lost without a cause, and others lost through the weeds because they refused to say YES to the shift! Unfortunately, they failed to realize that there's Power in the "Yes!"

Do you realize your Yes has the power to unlock some of the greatest treasures that have been locked up inside of you for years? What if I told you that I was sent to challenge you to break through whatever fears may be stopping you from saying "yes" to your next big opportunity or just a simple invitation to connect with some amazing people.

Have you ever rejected opportunities that could have changed the trajectory of your life because you refused to say *Yes*? Don't worry; you're not alone; I've been there and done that. The word *yes* not only comes with freedom, but movement and energy are also connected to that three-letter word. It's time to take action and create some massive momentum with our *YES*! Saying *yes* takes you out of your comfort zones which are not always easy to move away from because, in your mind, that's your safe place. Everything has a purpose, and your *yes* is attached to it. I'm here to challenge you to say *yes* and welcome that new beginning you so deserve.

Isn't it funny how we're so quick to say "NO" to things that have purpose and are placed in our lives to help us grow and enhance our mindsets and so many other areas in our lives, but then we say "Yes" to so many unproductive relationships, places, and things?

Don't get me wrong, I'm not saying to say *Yes* to everyone or everything. Anything that goes against your beliefs or anything dangerous or illegal, no, ma'am, absolutely not. However, I am saying there's power in saying yes to new doors and new opportunities and experiences in this season of your life.

Do you often find yourself asking God these questions, "Does my life have a Purpose? Is this all there is to life? What's next in this season of my life? Of course, you have, and guess what? So have I. I come to share some Good News! 2022 is indeed the Year of the Woman! In this season, God is truly ordering the steps of his daughters. The question is, are you ready to Say Yes to Purpose? Are you prepared to say *Yes* to You? Are you ready to say *Yes* to what's next in your life?

We need to get into the habit of responding yes when the doors are open and a yes when God closes a door. Let's take a moment to tackle that spirit called FEAR, which is nothing more than the acronym: **F**alse, **E**vidence, **A**ppearing, **R**eal, or another acronym: **F**ace, **E**verything, **A**nd **R**un! Unfortunately, many of us have allowed this word to disable and cripple us from saying yes to not only purpose but to so many things in life. I will be the first to admit there are many fears that we all may face when it comes to saying Yes to life, to purpose, to relationships, to our dreams, to your health, our careers, to our families, to ministry, to business, and even to yourself. One of the biggest fears is the fear of failure. We all may fall at some point and time, but the power and ability to get up lies within you. Today we are going to give ourselves permission, and we will no longer allow excuses to rob us from saying Yes ever again.

Let me ask you a few questions. What value do you want to add to the world? What have you been called to share? What have you been called to change? Who are you called to inspire?

Why not now, and why not YOU, I ask? It's time to say *YES* to You. Bet on You! It's time to get your mind right! Mindset is everything. I sense that many of you have been praying and asking God to send you a word or sign to confirm what you know he's already told you to do! If that's you...here's the only confirmation you need. You heard from God, and it's time to say *yes* and take action!

If need be, give yourself permission to rearrange some things and remember to enjoy the journey. When saying yes, most times than not, there will be some frustrations, unproductive days, all-nighters, and sometimes you may even want to simply give up along the way. This isn't failure; it's merely a part of the process in your journey.

Hey, Sis, let's kill the excuses and be the woman we were born to be for such a time as this! When you decide to move forward, you're letting go of all excuses. Today we will say yes to more and stop making excuses and make it happen. Please note that every YES will not be easy, and it may even take a great deal of sacrifice, but the reward will be worth it all. Yes, there will be good days and bad days, but it's all going to make sense in a minute.

We can all agree that it's easier to say No and acknowledge failure and defeat; however, if we are created in the image of God, then we were born to be fulfilled in every area of our lives. Let's get out of our own way and silence the voices in our heads that are constantly telling us that we don't deserve more; the devil is a **WHOLE LIE**! Today we say YES to all that God has in store for us. For the plan that He has for each and every one of us is for good and not for evil to give us a future and a hope and an expected in,, according to the Bible in Jeremiah 29:11.

Today we cancel all stinking thinking, and we prepare our hearts and minds as we say Yes to new beginnings. Saying yes causes us to respond and act. Listed below are 5 Principles that I want to share with you to say *Yes*.

5 Principles To Saying *Yes*

Let It Go
You can't move forward and go backward at the same time; it's impossible. Let go of the Past. Remember, whatever you feed will live, and whatever you starve will die. Make a decision today to starve the distractions of your past, according to Philippians 3:13-14.

Change Your Circle
Sometimes it's simply time to shift gears and change your environment and your relationships, especially if

they are no longer serving you and your purpose in life. I'm a firm believer that if it's costing you your peace, then it's too expensive. The Bible clearly tells us to lay aside every weight, and many times this includes unhealthy relationships (Hebrews 12:1).

Shift Your Mindset

It's important what you believe and who you believe. It's even more important as to what you think about yourself. Philippians 4:8 says whatsoever things are true, honest, just, or pure, think on these things. It's time to let go of all toxicity and Say Yes to Purpose. Yes, you can do anything you set your mind to accomplish. What your mind perceives, the mind achieves.

Forgiveness Is Key

I can't stress the importance of forgiveness. Not only is it an important factor in your health, but it's also important to your growth, opportunities, and relationships. You can't begin a new chapter in life until you have completely closed the door to your past. Forgiveness is a choice…Today choose to forgive. The spirit of unforgiveness will cause you to miss your purpose. Don't stay stuck; forgive to Live! Release it and let it go!!

Set Goals

Think about the results that you've been longing to see. Breathe and focus on one goal at a time. Create an action plan that is doable, and then jump into action. Discipline is key, and give yourself a timeline for achieving large goals. Plan for the future of your dreams. Ready, Set, GO!!

I celebrate you as you Say Yes to God, Family, Love, Joy, Life, Collaborations, Romance, Business, Ministry, Vacation, Dreams, Confidence, Purpose, Peace, Money, Happiness, Education, Marriage, Prayer, Faith, New Ideas, Success, Wealth, Health, New Mindset, Courage, Rest, Forgiveness, Miracles, Hope, New Friendships and more importantly Sis Say YES TO YOU!! Move out of your own way and get in the zone...**THE YES ZONE!**

In conclusion, take a moment and close your eyes. I want you to breathe in. Now I want you to release that breath. With your eyes still closed, imagine how much happier your life would be with this simple three-letter word called "YES." Life is short, and your children, spouse, family member, coworker, friend, boss, and even a stranger could be waiting on your yes. No longer will we continue to look back on our lives regretting over the things we woulda, coulda, and shoulda done. The time is NOW! Whoever you are and whatever side of the tracks you come from, always remember you are not too old, and it's not too late to say Yes. This is 2022, and you owe it to yourself! Your "YES" is waiting on your arrival...Let's Go!

About Prophetess LaKeisha J. Richards

Mildly put, LaKeisha J. Richards is a Powerhouse! Her titles are many. Amongst them are: Bestselling Author, Prophetess, Ordained Minister, CEO, Certified Life Coach, Christian Chaplain, and Ambassador of the highly acclaimed platform "Don't Give up on Love 2.0." She has achieved many more amazing milestones, including having sung background for the legendary Pastor Shirley Caesar, the late Reverend F.C. Barnes, and Brenda Whitfield Ellis. This wonderful Pastor's kid is also Former Dean of Administration to the Chancellor at Global Oved Seminary & University. She was blessed with the opportunity to participate in the Avon Voices Singing Contest in 2012; she has ministered in Revivals, Women Conferences, Youth Revivals, Single Conferences, Prayer Breakfasts, Jails, and in the Prisons.

LaKeisha is an alumnus of Dudley's Cosmetology University of Kernersville, NC, and has been a licensed cosmetologist for over 19 years. In 2000, she received a Certificate of Appreciation from the State of North Carolina Department of Correction for her voluntary work and ministry in the prison. In 1997, 2013, LaKeisha became an Ordained Minister under the leadership of Apostle Dr. Virginia Smith, who is also her mother. withIn 2013, she also became an ordained minister with The International Congress of Churches & Ministers, which was is under the leadership of Dr. Michael Chitwood. In 2019, LaKeisha was also recognized as an Iconic Woman in Ministry. LaKeisha received a diploma in Christian Chaplaincy from GODSU in May 2021.

LaKeisha's heart is truly that of a servant. Her influence on the lives of those around her is palpable. The love and genuine concern for the individuals she touches is astounding. What is most amazing, though, is through meeting this woman of God, most wouldn't ascertain her many accomplishments right away. She wears humility like a garment.

In her lifetime, this mother of two sons and grandmother to twin boys has faced many battles. One of the most significant ones was being diagnosed with a rare form of Ovarian cancer in June of 2010. Where many would have lost hope, she kept her faith. Through the grace of God, Lakeisha underwent two major surgeries within a short 2-month period. Through faith and prayer, by January 2011, she was cleared of cancer! This amazing victory launched LaKeisha even further into ministry.

     LaKeisha is a professional speaker and coach on the John Maxwell Team. She has also made appearances on Dominion TV and The Fierce, Ignition & Activation Radio Show with Apostle Deborah Allen. She has been featured in KISH Magazine (nominated on the 'Top 25 Global Influencer' list and Top 24 Women Who Win list), Kishma George Radio Show, and the Nicole LIVE Radio Show. She has been featured in magazine issues with Actor Jocelyn Castor, Dr. Joseph, and Pastor Lynette Dutton, Reality TV Star Lateshia Pearson, Evelyn Braxton (Tamar Braxton's Mother), Gospel Great Todd Dulaney, and Actor Denise Boutte from the movie Why Did I Get Married by Tyler Perry just to name a few. LaKeisha has also been featured in the Global Oved Seminary & University, EmpowerU Magazine, and a Co-Host on the Global Oved Seminary & University Teach and Pray Show.

     She is a role model to women everywhere and encourages all to walk in forgiveness and receive their healing. Her life is fully surrendered to the Lord. From having Cancer to being Homeless...LaKeisha J. Richards is not only a Survivor but one of "God's Leading Ladies" for such a time as this!

LaKeisha resides in North Carolina. With her mission clear, she continues to serve faithfully in ministry. Her platform, "Don't Give Up on Love 2.0," is available on all her social media sites. She also has several books that can be purchased.

To contact her for speaking engagements, contact her at: www.ljrichards.com or on her various social media platforms.

Stepping Out Of The Shadows
By Sandra Hale

As I sit and think about my life journey, I didn't know my worth and often wondered, why me? God, where are you? Life during the struggle seems unfair, but if you are reading this, that means you made it! You are on the right path; no need to feel as though you missed out. That is the devil's lie to keep you immobile, spinning in your self-imposed regret and having a pity party of one. Your thoughts are the driver in the midst of any situation, and they can hold you hostage and destroy your will to keep moving forward with your dreams.

Change what you are saying to the Masterpiece Visibly Positioned (MVP) of your life "YOU." Know that what you think about yourself can destroy and discourage you. Choose to switch lanes and start speaking life on this journey. Be proud of the lady in the mirror who survived the desert. Just like you, I had to make the decision to start doing what is necessary for my dreams. What God planted in us must be nurtured, cultivated, and shared. I am an overcomer, a gladiator who has learned to adjust for any battle. All our battles may not be won, but we are strong enough to survive through Jesus Christ. Step out of the shadows of others' opinions, comments, and passive-aggressive statements. Step out of the shadows of your disbelief in you. Come on, queen! It is your time to rise from the background and shine! It is time to open your heart and accept God's purpose-designed for you.

When God made you, He picked a birth date because He knew that the world needed you. It is time to make this next season about you. I know you think that it's selfish. Remember, you are God's MVP. It is necessary for women to intentionally leave space for themselves to seek purpose. How long are we going to keep our dreams shelved? How do you expect your dreams to grow if you never open up and let the light of belief shine in?

Stop the negative self-talk. Yes, you're busy, tired, and not feeling confident. You are a gladiator worthy of all God has prepared for you. I feel a need to celebrate because you are "STILL STANDING!" Life is not over. It is not selfish to give yourself some much-needed love and mercy. My friend, embrace and manifest your dreams. Destiny is calling you to your purpose. A new start is always possible. Stop allowing your past to determine your future.

I had to start intentionally focusing on my future. I was stuck feeling sorry for myself. I was stuck reflecting on the things from my past that I couldn't change. I was stuck in the "church hurt" that I had accepted as truth. I chose to embrace and nurture the hurt and allowed it to grow. Our pasts are set in stone.

We can't go back to fix a mistake, right a wrong, or make changes. But we can use our memories of the past to support our future. We can use what we went through to help heal our maimed hearts so that we can rise to help someone else.

Who would have thought a small-town country girl, beginning elementary school surrounded by the environment of prejudice in our township, as one of two little black girls in the community would be here? I am the five-year-old who no one would sit next to at school or on the bus. I am the little girl that no one would hold hands with because of the color of her skin. I am the girl who stood alone at recess every day because no one would play with me. I am the young one that began to make herself throw up at the bus stop to avoid going to school. I am the young lady that was the only black girl in her high school graduating class.

That entire experience of kindergarten through twelfth grade planted a seed in me of rejection that birthed self-hatred and cultivated a shy, withdrawn young woman who grew up needing to be accepted, heard, loved, and needed to be protected. Through my relationship with my awesome Father, Jesus Christ, I learned that all of life's experiences are valuable and needed for my destiny. Every day that we open our eyes is a gift given to react positively on purpose. Be determined and stand up for yourself. You deserve to be free! Step out of the shadows of your pain, set your goals, and get accountability. We still have time! Your call to action is to focus and move forward! Your future begins with you believing in you! You can free yourself by turning the page, standing firm, and writing your future.

Do not let the past hurts stop you. Instead, use the past to gain momentum to stand for you. I had to release myself from the bondage of unforgiveness. Unforgiveness is like an ugly black leech that will suck the life out of you if it is not removed. Unforgiveness leaves you vulnerable and stuck. Unforgiveness is a breeding ground for bondage that will delay your purpose. Let the drawbridge down, queen, and come out from behind your walls of protection. Those past experiences have taken up enough valuable living space. Forgive and let it go. It is time to be free. Your future is purposeful. You may never receive an apology, but you can release the hurt and remnants of unforgiveness that have hindered you and served no purpose.

We are women stepping out of the shadows with self-worth. We are ready to dream, ready to live, ready to love ourselves, and intentionally use our heartstrings from life as strengths to grow and keep moving forward. I am a witness that it does not matter the good, bad, and ugly you were born into and lived through. God has a plan. With your first inhale as you entered this life, God released your destiny into your young spirit and sealed it with your cry out for life. Daughter, who you are is on purpose, ordained and planned by God. We come into this life with everything we need to support our destiny, protected and tucked away inside of us. We are birthed with purpose, and as we go through life, every struggle is a badge of honor that you survived to support your mission, your call, your destiny. It is not too late to dream and live on purpose. Take one of the most important steps and believe that you have purpose. You are here at this very moment for a reason, and it is your job to learn, grow and surround yourself with people who are ignited.

    I felt like I missed my time to dream and that I had no purpose. I had to stop thinking about what I had not done and started telling myself "I can," "I will," and "I shall." I had to remember who God said I am and step out of the shadows of all that negative self-talk. What we say out of our month is a direct reflection of what is in our heart. I am better, I am empowered, I am equipped, and I am still standing! There are so many dreams and visions that are stagnant and left dormant because of fear and disbelief in our abilities that God breathed into us at birth. I had to flood myself with positivity and start the process of freeing myself from the fortress I built to protect myself from any future hurt and pain. How awesome it is to come out and feel God's breeze, sunshine, rain, and snow on my face. I was a captive of my own negative self-talk. Don't be so hard on yourself. It is ok to choose you. Yes, friend!! I see your head lifting already. Come on out and encourage yourself. You are worth it!

    It is time to shift! We will no longer shrink into the crowd! Women often hide how we really feel with our false illusions of happiness when facing our peers, but here we are left feeling overwhelmed, stressed, and disappointed with where we are in life. We often find ourselves not seeking God for direction but just accepting where we are in our unfulfilled life and going with the flow. We were created to support, but not at the expense of delaying our purpose. So often, we forget to make ourselves a priority. We fail to encourage ourselves. We dim our light to make others shine and forget that our hopes and dreams are important. Your personal fulfillment adds to your overall wellness, so lift yourself up, be grateful, happy, and fulfilled.

I can't remind everyone enough to believe that you have what it takes. Speak positively to that scared person inside who is ready. That purpose in you is bubbling up like a volcano ready to erupt. Your purpose is at the finish line waiting for you. Don't let nerves, self-doubt, smother and push your destiny any further down inside of you. All those dreams and visions are ready to be out front and free. Let's shift out of looking back, no more shrinking into the crowd. It is ok to put the spotlight on ourselves, stand tall and let the purpose of your life blossom. Being fulfilled in life with God should be our number one goal because when a woman is happy and confident, everyone connected to her will benefit.

As women, we often feel guilty when we start trying to care for our needs, wants, and desires. Fulfillment is rewarding, whether it is fun, travel, work, relationships, or other activities. Ultimately, we all seek fulfillment in everything that we do. You are longing for more, and a great place to start is providing yourself fulfillment through making time for yourself and being grateful for all that you have survived. Get quiet with God, encourage yourself, and listen. Start your day being intentional; no more shrinking into the crowd. Step out of the shadows, forgive, and let go of the fear, self-doubt, shyness, and negative talk. Keep moving forward because your possibilities are endless. Your purpose is tucked within waiting to be stirred up, waiting to be uncovered, and waiting for permission to serve.

As women, our heartstrings of life hold everything we have been through. Our heartstrings can hold us, hostage, halted, stuck, or scared or they can propel, inspire, and drive you forward. We should not try to cover up, change or hide what we have been through because our heartstrings are the core of who we were born to be. Every life experience plays a role in forming who we are as women. Be proud and embrace all that makes you laugh, pray, cry, hurt, and grow. Accept that you are unique! The heartstrings of life are our stepping stones to greatness! Heartstrings nourish, connect, push, collect, and hold vitality. Know that we are daughters *with the promise*, not a daughter *looking for promise*. God is Consistent; He provides His grace is enough, His love never fails. "For I know the plans I have for you," says the Lord. "They are plans for good and not for disaster, to give you a future and a hope." (Jeremiah 29:1 NIV)

We must learn to maintain a rich, balanced life throughout each transitional phase that we are faced with. You, my friend, have spent enough years unfulfilled. Awesome job, mom, wife, caregiver, aunt, sister, niece, grandmother, and co-worker. Now it is time for you to start the work that will release the hidden treasures God tucked away within you at birth. Do not be limited by what you see; believe, close your eyes, and activate your blind faith by listening to God's voice. Move when He says move. God has so much prepared that you will not see; blind faith just keeps stepping out of the shadows. Whatever your purpose is, you were born because it needs to be carried out by you.

I speak life to your new season! Now it is time for you to start the work that will release the hidden treasures God tucked away within. Take a deep breath and exhale to release those treasures and step out of the shadows. You made it through all the valleys of deception, mountains of struggle, hills of stress, desert storms of turmoil, and every complicated situation you were in. Some did not survive, but here you are with all your battle scars of life! Look in the mirror at that strong gladiator looking back at you. Smile and believe You Are The BOMB! You are the next woman destined to use her heartstrings of life to rise above and soar. Welcome, we have been waiting for you!

About Sandra Hale

Sandra Hale stands as an overcomer who learned through the challenges and victories of her life that our possibilities are limitless. A leader, trainer, strategist, coach, author, wife, and mother, she has been married for thirty-seven years, with three amazing adult children and two grandchildren. Sandra believes that your career is not a lasting sign of success; it is your family legacy that lives to tell your story.

Sandra is a thirty-year career financial management analyst who has many achievements and awards. She has a calm disposition that stands strong during the storm and enables her to see solutions that lead to greater possibilities. She is highly regarded as an expert who mentors, sets goals, determines actions to achieve the goals, and mobilizes resources to execute the actions. As an advisor, her peers and leadership team rely on her to plan how the ends will be achieved with the resources provided.

Sandra's purpose has been birthed, and she is now stepping out of the shadows. Her passion for helping women who feel they are stuck in the cycles of their life, unable to believe they can take the steps necessary to achieve greatness, is what drives her. She trains and inspires women to believe in themselves, dream again, and walk in the freedom of being unique. She believes that it is necessary for us to learn to maintain a rich, balanced life throughout each transitional phase that we are faced with. Sandra is driven to awaken the gift of purpose that is waiting to erupt in us all; it is not too late!

Website: www.sandrahale.com
Email: ItsSandrahale@gmail.com
IG: @itssandrahale FACEBOOK: Sandrahale

My Emotional Trauma Almost Took Me Out

By Michelle Alston

As I sit in my writing lab surrounded by the vibrant colors of teal, orange-yellow and red. I was listening to the sounds of the cars scrolling down the road and the rain knocking on my window. My mind wandered with the excitement of what was going on around me, almost as if those millions of dollars checks were in my hands. Hey, don't mind me just dreaming out loud. Because so many years, I have hidden and cried to myself that my dreams were hidden behind all the emotional trauma I have encountered over the years.

Abandoned, rejected, and abused physically, mentally, sexually, and emotionally have caused me to think little of myself at the time that I did not want to live anymore. I was a teen mom at 14 years old, searching for love in places I should have never been. I was now in my head because now a 17 year old mom of three, although one was aborted. After all, my mom said not again, so turning 18 was her avenue to say goodbye and don't come back. They said she was joking but proved it was not a joke as she never came to see about me. What parent would leave a child or teach them how to handle the real world of life.

All the trauma I have encountered throughout my childhood haunted me as a nightmare every night. I couldn't sleep. The dreams would not stop. I had to make it. I would make something out of life cause they all threw me away and out like trash. High school dropout on welfare food stamps was not enough to build or buy my dream because one day, I knew I was going to make it; I had hope and had to make my nightmare into goals because everyone counted me out. They said I would never be anything; they said I was not good enough. People only came around when they needed something, which was not good enough.

I have lost myself and have now tapped back into the life I was meant to live but wait a minute, I had to sacrifice a lot to see this moment. It all had to happen so I could see these days of the greatness that was hidden behind all the silent cries. The mental breakdown is sitting in the dark—the shameful and embarrassing moment of shame to ask for help. I am human, and I do not have to impress anyone anymore. I had done just what my heart had encouraged me to do: get up and move. I owe it to my children, grandchildren, and God's kids. They deserve the best version of me.

Pastor D told me many years ago to stop letting people dump their garbage in my yard and leave it all a mess, not even offering to help clean it up or put it back. I never listened; my mind, emotion, and heart were full of other people's junk. I was everything to and for everyone and felt I was nothing to nobody. I finally realized that I needed help when everyone I cared about left me. Growing up, I never felt the love and the care from family. I never thought I belonged. I built my family with people in my community that showed love for my children and me. My family was also my church family. They taught me how to love because love was the key there. Even if it was not real, they showed love.

On this journey called life, there are some things we will have to learn to control if we want to become successful dreamers and move to purpose. Through all I have been through, I have learned to seek help to grow spiritually, emotionally, and mentally. I had to have control of my mind and feeling. I begin to pray and read more, seeking the presence of God in my life. My favorite story in the bible during this time of my life was the story of Job because he lost everything and never fussed or cussed at God; we will lose a dollar and go crazy. During the wildest moment of my life, I stopped asking why and began to cry. Forgive me, Lord. Then I put into practice seven-step that helped me control the emotional trauma that was trying to take me out before my time but GOD.

Step One: Acknowledge the Trauma

To begin my healing process, I had first to acknowledge that I have been through something that was causing pain in my life, and I will no longer suppress my pain to save someone else feeling. You have to acknowledge and accept your experience as a reality; know you do not deserve to be hurt by it, and take the necessary steps towards healing. It would help if you acknowledged how your past had impacted your life to move forward with positive change. If you want help understanding what happened beyond everyday human experience, please consult a professional specialist specializing in this area, such as an emotion-focused therapist.

Step Two: Know your triggers

It is essential to understand what brings you back to the traumatic experience(s) and triggers symptoms of emotional trauma. It is necessary to journal about your experiences and any triggers that you identify to understand better yourself and the things that may bring up difficult emotions or memories. Doing so will help you become more aware of what to avoid and provide insight on what might help manage difficult symptoms. If avoidance is a strategy you have used in the past to cope with your emotional trauma, know that it only keeps the pain trapped inside, which will continue to affect your daily life negatively. Experiencing reminders of traumatic events can be very painful, but it is necessary to start the healing process. In time, the intensity of the symptoms will become less, and you will manage them more effectively.

Step Three: Seek help

It is widespread for people who have experienced emotional trauma to feel ashamed, embarrassed, or like they are the only ones who have gone through something so difficult. It is essential to understand that you are not alone and that help is available. Talk to someone you trust about what you are experiencing, whether a friend, family member, or therapist. Sharing your story can be an incredibly healing experience and will help you start the process of healing from emotional trauma. If talking about your experiences is too difficult at first, consider writing them down in a journal. This can also help identify triggers and understand how the traumatic experience has affected your life.

Step Four: Prayer changes things

It can be tough to come out of a traumatic experience feeling like God is still there with you. It might seem impossible at first, but it is essential to know that he will always love and accept you no matter how low you feel. Even when our lives are filled with pain, Jesus suffered more than any human ever has or will. The most powerful thing we have on Earth is a prayer that allows us to communicate directly with the Creator who loves us unconditionally! When praying about your experiences, consider asking for strength in understanding what happened without judgment, guidance on how to heal from emotional trauma through Christ's finished work on the cross so that he may give you a new life free from struggle and pain while drawing closer towards Him daily as your source of strength and joy. Whether you are struggling with emotional trauma or simply feeling the weight of life on your shoulders, take comfort in knowing that there is always hope through God's unconditional love!

Step Five: Forgive yourself and others

Forgiving yourself is crucial in the process of healing from emotional trauma. If you are having trouble doing so, it may help to talk to someone who can give you support and understanding during this time. Forgiveness does not mean that what happened was okay or should be forgotten; instead, forgiveness means letting go of anger which only keeps us stuck in pain while allowing God's love into our hearts! We all make mistakes, but there comes a time when we must forgive ourselves for them and those who have hurt us because no matter how much they might deny their actions, Jesus desires complete restoration between both parties through His death on the cross. He wants nothing more than for everyone to come home where true joy awaits us.

Even if we have difficulty forgiving someone, God's love never fails and always waits for us to return home through His Son Jesus!

Step Six: Self-care is important

It is widespread for people who have experienced emotional trauma to neglect their own needs. This can lead to feelings of isolation, sadness, and anxiety. It is important to remember that self-care is not selfish! Taking care of yourself by doing things you enjoy, getting enough sleep, eating healthy foods, and spending time with loved ones will help you feel better mentally and emotionally.

Step Seven: Now walk it out

The final step in healing from emotional trauma is walking it out. This means taking the steps necessary to live a healthy and fulfilling life, despite what you have been through. This may include seeking counseling, participating in support groups, getting a life coach, or attending church services. It also includes setting boundaries with those who have hurt you in the past and moving on toward your future dreams and goals!

Remember that you are not alone in this journey, no matter how difficult it might be. God loves you and will never leave your side!

In conclusion.

This is not the season for a microwave attitude. Healing from any trauma takes time. In the same way, a microwave can cause interference with your communication devices. A microwave attitude can interfere with your personal growth. Nobody is perfect but God, and we must learn to live a life fearing God and not people, places, or things. It is possible to heal from emotional trauma when you can't see your way out. The steps have been outlined to provide a foundation for healing. However, it is essential to note that everyone's journey is unique, and no microwave process can help you heal fast. You must create a toolbox that enables you to overcome your pain. Listen, these battles that we fight in this life are not for us but for us as believers to share and encourage the world that the God we serve will not put more on you than you can bear. So, seek help before it's too late, and never allow the trials in this life to silence you during the storm that enters your path. Your pain was not for you. It is for someone else to heal from the pain you have already recovered from. It's a new day, so let us move and be free, no turning back. Be gentle with yourself, take things at your own pace, and allow yourself to experience the healing process in whatever way feels best for you. I pray you find peace, hope, and joy in moving toward your goals and dreams.

MICHELLE ALSTON

About Michelle Ann Alston

Michelle Alston is the CEO and Founder of Mtugi Monae LLC, Mtugi Monae was created from a passion to serve the community. Michelle has been in public service for over 10 years and now serving as a social service rep in the District of Columbia government. Michelle spent four years as a Career Agent motivating, facilitating peer groups, and creating workshops topics that will empower the low-income community to find work or finish school. Michelle's lifetime philosophy is to create and develop a solid foundation both professionally and personally. The other one is that everyone needs a plan and purpose in order not to flip flop through life.

As a domestic violence survivor, homelessness, high school dropout, single parent, Grandma, Godmother, and friend. Michelle's desire to encourage family and loved ones to seek help when they have fallen into the difficult barrier in life. Michelle's past has motivated her to give to others in need that she did not get.

Michelle has taken the pressure from her past and turned it into her success story. Michelle received her high school diploma from night school. Graduated with her Associate and Bachelor of Science degree from Southeastern University and Master of Arts degree from Strayer University. Michelle is also one of the Co-authors of the low-income female entrepreneur project (L.I.F.E. project). Michelle has received multiple community service awards from organizations that serve the community. As an inspiring Motivational Speaker, Model, and life coach, Michelle desires to lead with excellence, motivate with class, train with integrity, and serve underserved communities.

Contact Michelle:
Michelle Alston Facebook
Michelle Ann Linkin
@Mtugimone2 Instagram
mtugimonae@gmail.com

Discover your Limiting Beliefs and Strengthen your Relationships
By Giselle Vazquez

Imagine what a perfect marriage looks like. Who is your partner? What are their interests? What is their occupation? Then ask yourself if you have similarities to that? Do you see your marriage as the perfect fairytale ending? Do you see yourself overcoming challenges together and evolving with one another? And if you are currently married, did your marriage turn out as you imagined?

Growing up, I lived in what most would say is a broken household with no father present. I yearned for the day that I would have a family with both parents present. Unfortunately for me, I never got the opportunity, so I began to imagine my future life as a wife with kids. This vision evolved as I watched all the happy ending Disney fairytales. Through these movies, I witnessed that happy endings do happen even through all the hard times.

Once I met my now husband, I felt like I was swept off my feet by Prince Charming and was on cloud nine. I was saved from the chaos and disconnection of my childhood home. I was madly in love and enjoyed every chance I had to be with him. Then came marriage and children! I was so excited now that I finally had the family I always wanted growing up. Oh, but how I was wrong. A few years into our marriage, my husband decided to join the United States Marine Corps. After his initial training, I was hit with a rude awakening. I noticed a difference in his demeanor that was worrisome. And instead of confronting the situation, I choose to adapt to the new him. This is where I began losing the essence of myself and my ability to set boundaries.

Then came deployments, and, well, let's just say that our connection with one another had almost fully diminished. I was distant and felt alone. Inside I blamed the Corps. I played the "what if" scenarios in my head time and time again, creating even more distance in our relationship. Fast forward a few years, when we moved back to our hometown, we were on the verge of divorce and in complete rage toward one another. I was depressed and suicidal. I did not understand why this was happening to me! My family was breaking apart right before my eyes. What was the point? I worked so hard to keep our family together, losing myself in the process, and now I was losing it all!

At that moment, I chose victimhood. I chose to feel pity for what was happening to me, and I made sure the world saw it through my actions. Then God sent me an angel in physical form. My angel showed me there are more ways to see things, there are more ways to do things, and best of all, I had complete control of it. That is when I learned that I had been doing married life all wrong. I was trying to control the situation vs. controlling the underlying cause, ME! I realized that I had to first focus on myself for my marriage to be successful. My spiritual, mental, and physical self. It's like when a plane is crashing, and you have to put your oxygen mask on first before you can help with anyone else's.

Once I began focusing on myself, everything else fell in alignment. I changed my perspective and belief about what marriage looks like and how it works. I began to change how I spoke and set appropriate boundaries for myself. From there, everything else followed suit or shifted out of my life. I cannot say it was easy, but it was worth every moment. My husband then followed suit as I rebuilt myself, reclaimed my feminine power, and honored everyone on their journey. He saw my growth and desired the same in his life.

As you begin to analyze your life and decide what you desire, you will realize that you can only change what you have control over, yourself. Things will become easier to handle. You will better understand your situation and everyone involved from the shift in your viewpoint. This takes you looking deep into your belief systems and your vision. What you envision comes from a set of belief systems you have come to establish from your experiences growing up, your environment, and even your religious upbringing. Belief is an acceptance that something is true. This can pertain to religion, and individual perspectives, such as word phrases like money doesn't grow on trees. That being said, we all have a set of beliefs we are programmed to, starting from the womb. On a day-to-day basis, this is how we make decisions at the subconscious level. It is a part of who we are, and it controls the way we perceive things.

So, going off the notion that money doesn't grow on trees, one may experience things like guilt if they receive money freely because they're out of alignment with their beliefs. The great thing about beliefs is that you have a choice to continue in the belief systems you were born into or change them. You can shift your beliefs in two different ways, first by an impactful event and second by constant spaced repetition. Constant spaced repetition is when you learn a new habit or new information in intervals to retain the habit or information easier and quicker. This is the most common method used by those in an awakened state seeking to change their habits for a different outcome. Now, what happens if you don't know how to? What if you continue to be faced with the challenges of the old way of thinking?

First, I would encourage you to analyze the results in your life. See if there is something that doesn't suit the direction you are pursuing. Once you have determined what that is, choose to change these habits that continue to give you these results. In the process of changing these habits, it will feel forced and unnatural. This is because it's something you have not done before, and it doesn't align with your current beliefs. You will need the dedication to stick to these new habits through constant spaced repetition. Once you have been consistent with this change, what was once a forced action then turns into habits of nature that align with a new belief. It will no longer feel forced; it will simply be an unconscious act.

We are all living in a hell of our own making. As we dream our biggest dreams and desires, we limit ourselves from the beliefs we took on from our parents, religion, and society. From these beliefs, we choose to evolve or continue to stick to them. The problem is that these beliefs limit us most of the time as we believe blindly. Think back to a time when you bought into a belief. What did it do to your dreams?

When I was younger, I experienced a lot of emotional and sexual abuse. From these experiences, I chose to believe I was unworthy and incapable of being loved. As I began to delve into my biggest desires, I found myself making progress just to be met with a brick wall. I was stuck in the two steps forward three steps back cycle time and time again. It wasn't until I began to work through my beliefs of unworthiness that I was able to shift my life into progression. Subsequently, I saw the blocks before hitting them, which allowed me to bust through them versus getting stuck. I claimed my power back and chose to believe in my worth. It first took borrowing the beliefs that others had in me, but with the encouragement of my coaches, I was able to adopt their belief in me for myself.

I have since dedicated myself to helping military spouses build stronger connections through all the chaotic transitions by reclaiming their power and being whole first. I provide the tools to clarify, fortify and amplify their love so that their legacy can be built on the strong foundation of their duality.

I have come to understand that marriages are not all candy and roses. They are not like the Disney Fairytales. It's not always as we imagine, but it is worth every second, especially when you have two individuals who are on their separate journeys, willing and ready to come together to support one another—creating a duality of marriage, where two individuals form a unity becoming each other's ying to their yang.

So, I go back and ask what beliefs are you choosing to buy into that have limited your progression in life? Is there a belief that you have blocking the connection within your marriage or other relationships? If so, choose to recognize the habits you have formed based on these beliefs that are holding you back. Once you have, choose to change them because you have been gifted with talents to share with the world. You have been put on this earth with a purpose on purpose, and you should not be stuck in the hell that these limiting beliefs have kept you in. Be free and liberate yourself into the grandest heavens you deserve. Cherish your life, cherish your relationships. You matter in this world. Believe it and proclaim it. If it's hard for you, then borrow my belief in you. I see your light even at its dimmest point. Go in nature, recharge, and shine bright.

GISELLE VAZQUEZ

About Giselle Vazquez

Giselle Vazquez is a native of Puerto Rico (a U.S commonwealth state) who moved to Florida on the U.S. mainland at the age of one. As a preteen, her family moved to Utah, where she currently resides with her loving husband, a U.S.M.C. Combat Veteran, and their five adorable children.

Giselle worked as an early childhood special education teacher. As a result of teaching children with special needs, she found that her passion was not only to help children with special needs find their strengths but to help them improve their quality of life.

Combining the tools she gained in her teaching experience and also as a military wife, Mrs. Vazquez started an initiative to help military wives during their spouses' deployments, from emotional support to natural birthing support.

Mrs. Vazquez is a dedicated Warrior's Connection & Mindset Coach who loves exploring nature and chasing after waterfalls. She operates a personal security detail and firearms training company with her husband, along with a coaching company, InfinitCor.

Currently, she helps veterans and their spouses who are struggling with their union win the war within their relationship by providing them the tools to clarify, fortify, and amplify their love and legacy. If you know any military family that needs this kind of support, her books are filled with resources and honors those seeking stronger relationships.

With the purchase of this book, you may book a FREE discovery session with Giselle, and walk away with a three-step plan for a successful relationship. Reach out through one of her social media platforms below.

Warrior Connections And Mindset Couch | Personal Discovery Coach | Speaker And Author

Social Media:
https://www.facebook.com/giselle.ivette.vazquez
https://www.facebook.com/gisellejumps
https://www.instagram.com/gisellejumps/
https://www.tiktok.com/@gisellejumps

Life Challenges... Just Stepping Stones Working For My Good
By Mary Davis

To grandmothers, aunties, and all who raise *children you did not birth*, it's not about you. We are strong women put on this earth to multitask—your voice matters. No job is too big or too small as long as you depend on God. No matter the stumbling blocks that come your way, it is working for your good. It ignites me to see someone I helped along this journey by empowering them with resources and scripture to change their lives and bring value to them. My mission is to educate people on the importance and purpose of insurance, especially life insurance.

My story begins with my passion for helping people, and advocating in the 80s with Acorn against injustice for the homeless. Securing vacant homes to house them was endless. I had to find resources that I could refer others to, as well as myself. I would be that person, and I wanted to bring value to my friends and family in the Community.

While on this journey, life hit a somewhat average family. My worst nightmare hit, my child was experimenting with drugs, and I did not know what to do or who to turn to. Not my family. There was a mother, father, and siblings; we were fine – so I thought. We were active in church, so naturally, I turned to my pastor, who could not help with referrals. I was resentful of the situation I was in. God sent a street ministry to save her and me. Family and onlookers could not help us. It took someone who had been there and understood her addiction. They were sent to save my family from the blame game. They took her and ministered to her, and she received the Holy Spirit.

I had a smile all the time but was broken and ashamed, so my other kids were somewhat neglected; I was worried all the time. I found out that I needed a personal relationship with God to find help. Sure, I was in church, but it was for a get together to see and travel, but not to heal. I began to recognize that I needed to have a relationship with God and with the Holy Spirit. I was baptized again at Bethesda, filled with the Holy Ghost speaking in tongues. I thought that my problem was over.

I became a young grandmother at the age of 36. Wow, what am I going to do? What will people say? I felt ashamed that my child had a child. Where did we go wrong as parents? I felt my life was over. Then more children came, and I became a foster parent. I have a new family; I can't do it. But God – God kept her. The children finished school and great-grands to date. We are so grateful that God kept us. The grandkids were a blessing, do not use them as an excuse.

I realized that I needed to fall on my face with my father and study the Word instead of reading it. The Word got in me; I started being afraid of not obeying God's word. As long as I thirsted for Him and needed more of Him, He directed my path. God had a plan for me, and He does for you, no matter how long it takes.

Do not stop working toward your dreams because of setbacks. Life challenges come with setbacks, and you are in store for a comeback. When you are older, you start to believe it's over; I missed it, and my dreams and goals are useless. You don't realize this is the beginning. Don't let others keep throwing your compass off. Thank God that He kept you around; it was not just to raise children; you are blessed and equipped to do it all.

Most grandparents/grannies are content and want to give up, live in a retirement facility, and be bored to death in similar situations, no matter what age. Grandparents, we have so much inside of us, wisdom, love, and purpose. I was blessed through it all; she is not dead to this day and enjoying her grandchildren. Grandparents have God embedded within them, and the world is waiting for the adventure you can take them on, and you can be independent and active.

It's not over; go back to the source, the Word of God. In Genesis 18:1-14, Sara thought it was over; God fulfilled the promise. Nothing is too hard for my God; He will show up at the appointed time. *Habakkuk 2:3 For the vision is yet for an appointed time, but at the end, it shall speak and not lie. Though it tarry, wait for it because it will surely come.*

As most of us do, the problem was that I quit during the challenge and gave up, feeling sorry for myself when in reality, the grandchildren were my *WHY*. You begin to listen to the naysayers and family that don't respect your dream but need you to run errands while they work.

You must believe and trust God. You must do the work. When life gives you a chance, take it. I was held by the promise and did not even know it. God will arrange and direct your path with or without your permission. We have a purpose; God guides and orders our steps at His will when we recognize it. Fear of failure will cripple you. *God did not give you a spirit of fear, but of power, love, and sound mind.* 2 Timothy:1:7.

Everything He promised is here this season; I can feel it; I cannot give up now; I've come too far from where I started from. The song says, "Even when I could not see him, He was working, and even when I could not feel Him, He was working. He never stopped making a way for me; now it's my turn again."

So, this is what you do despite your situation, do not sit at home and become stricken with diseases because you don't move around.

- You must have mental stimulation.
- avoid situations that hinder your condition. Get rid of your Jonah during the storm; you become what you talk about.

- Write your plan, Jeremiah 29:11 *For I know the plans I have for you, declares the Lord, plans to prosper you and not to harm you, plans to give you hope and a future.*
- Remember that you are worth it.
- We cannot refund our blessing.
- Read Battlefield of the Mind by Joyce Meyers.
- You cannot stay in your baggage.

Grandmothers live your life; God has work for you to do, no matter how old you are. I didn't think it was going to happen until I read it in The Book (Bible). I held on through trials, tribulation, and doubts; I had to go back to The Book. Everything you need, God's got it; not getting along at home, confusion in the house of God, it's in The Book.

If you lack anything, you can find it in The Book. Genesis 1, ask Him, not your friend. Read it for yourself and know that every gift comes from above. The operating instructions are right in front of you; it's in The Book.

I am a witness that if you forget Him, He is not going to remind you of what He has in store for you. He wants you to tap into Him and be the best you can be, His obedient servant serving Him and being a servant to His people. I have learned to thrive in a tainted atmosphere, and I am a change agent by being a lifter, influencer, and encourager.

About Mary Ellen Davis

Mary Ellen Davis is a native of Memphis, Tennessee, and a proud graduate of Hamilton High School. For over 40 years, she has dedicated her life as a servant, community advocate, and volunteer to the St. Louis community.

In the 1970s, she relocated to St. Louis, MO, obtained an Associate Degree in Diet Technology from St. Louis Community College of Florissant Valley, while raising a family, and volunteers in her community, . She began advocating with Acorn Housing for the homeless, which later inspired the Blessing Bag Initiative.

She is a 40-plus-year member of Mount Esther Missionary Baptist Church, a member of the Mass Choir, a Sunday School Teacher, and serves on the Trustee and Deaconess Board.

For over 25 years, Mary has been a member of the Federation of Block Units of Metropolitan. St. Louis, an auxiliary of the Urban League of Metropolitan St. Louis, where she has served as the Area F Council Chair for the 1st Ward, 2nd Ward, and the 27th Ward of St. Louis and is currently the Financial Secretary and Membership Committee Chair.

"With God's compass for me, this has all paid off. Now I am the newly elected Committeewoman of the 27th Ward, a better position to empower my constituents with valuable insight into how the city offices and how imperative their vote is. The people make the Community."

Davis has been awarded for exemplifying such dedication and devotion to the Saint Louis Community. She received the prestigious S.P. Stafford award from the Urban League of Metropolitan St. Louis, the Harper's Cup from the Federation of Block Units of Metropolitan St. Louis, and the Earl E. Howe Community Service Award from the 27th Ward. In 2020, she received Community Recognition from the Top Ladies of Distinction, Incorporated, and Special Recognition from Pastor Johnathan Lewis of the Saint

Mathew Lutheran Church of the 27th Ward for participation and support of their 120th Anniversary Celebration.

She continues to be a servant by becoming a licensed Life and Health Insurance agent and licensed in Fixed Annuities to offer financial literacy to the St. Louis families. Mary is an independent Representative of Primerica and a strong supporter of their mission to help people become debt-free, properly protected with insurance, and financially independent. She offers free literacy classes on building a financial house. Certified as a Mental Health First Aid Responder, she is able to support and better serve her Community. She is also a certified Senior health agent.

Family is important to Mary as she is a proud mother of four, Ardrea Allen, Fredrick S. Davis, Tara Davis Smith, Robert Davis Jr., and a proud grandmother of thirteen grandchildren and fifteen great-grandchildren. Mary's family time is spent attending Saturday brunches, playing games, and traveling with family, friends, and colleagues. Encouraging them to build a relationship with God, he will direct your path. *Psalm 37:3 Trust in the Lord and do good.*

Mary is a woman on a mission, always positioning herself to help others by providing empowering resources and information to anyone willing to receive them.

Contact Information:
Merryd543@gmail.com
314-825-0585

Made in the USA
Columbia, SC
26 September 2022